SUPER
privacy

STASHED   CONCEALMENT   SOLITUDE

SUPER
privacy

ISOLATION   SECRET   EXILE   RETREAT

SECLUSION   SAFE   RETIREMENT   HIDE

EXILE   RETIREMENT   SAFE   RETREAT

HIDE   SECLUSION   SAFE   RETIREMENT

CONCEALMENT   STASHED   SOLITUDE

ISOLATION   SECRET   EXILE   RETREAT

THE COMPLETE GUIDE TO PERSONAL PRIVACY AND FINANCIAL FREEDOM IN TOMORROW'S CASHLESS SOCIETY

BOB HAMMOND

PALADIN PRESS • BOULDER, COLORADO

HIDE   SECLUSION   SAFE   RETIREMENT

Super Privacy: The Complete Guide to Personal Privacy and Financial Freedom in Tomorrow's Cashless Society by Bob Hammond

Copyright © 1997 by Bob Hammond

ISBN 0-87364-920-6
Printed in the United States of America

Published by Paladin Press, a division of
Paladin Enterprises, Inc., P.O. Box 1307,
Boulder, Colorado 80306, USA.
(303) 443-7250

Direct inquiries and/or orders to the above address.

PALADIN, PALADIN PRESS, and the "horse head" design
are trademarks belonging to Paladin Enterprises and
registered in United States Patent and Trademark Office.

Contents

Warning

This book contains certain confidential information that could easily be subject to abuse or misuse. The author does not encourage, endorse, or recommend the use of any of these methods as a means to defraud or violate the rights of any individual or organization. The reader is therefore encouraged to be diligent in applying this information to specific situations. The author is not engaged in rendering any legal professional service. The services of a professional person are recommended if legal advice or assistance is needed. The author, publisher, and distributors of this book hereby disclaim any personal losses or liabilities caused by the use or misuse of any information presented herein. This book is presented *for academic study only.*

Author's Note

Foreword

After her divorce, Jan Johnson applied for a car loan. Her palms began to sweat as she waited for the finance manager to return with her credit report, knowing that her credit history was filled with collection accounts, charge-offs, and late payments. That was one of the reasons her marriage didn't work out—her ex-husband had difficulty holding on to a job, and they struggled with constant financial problems.

The manager returned with a smile on his face. Jan could hardly believe her ears when he told her that the loan had been approved. Later she discovered that as a result of her address change and return to her maiden name, the credit bureau was unable to locate her old file and the report said, "No Record

Found." Because of her income, solid employment history, and substantial down payment, the loan was approved—in spite of her lack of credit history.

Jan began to apply for credit cards and loans from a variety of creditors. All of her applications were approved until one day when a clerk asked her a simple question. Based on Jan's reply, the clerk ran another credit report. The information from Jan's old file was picked up and merged with her new file (which until now contained only positive entries). Jan's application for credit was denied. Once again, her credit rating was ruined.

If only Jan had read *Super Privacy*. She would have realized that she had accidentally stumbled across a method of alternate identity that could have set her free from the bondage of her (and her former husband's) past credit history. With the proper understanding of the system, she could have easily avoided having her old file merged with her new one. Armed with the proper information, Jan could have started over with a clean slate.

In another situation, a couple in southern California was turned down for a mortgage on a new home as a result of a previous judgment on their credit report. They came to me for a consultation, desperate for a way to reestablish their credit within a short period of time. After listening to their story and reviewing their credit reports, I told them about a little-known technique for legally creating an alternate credit file. A few weeks later, they invited me to a housewarming at their new $500,000 home.

* * *

Super Privacy begins where other books on personal finance leave off. Rather than dwelling on long, drawn-out techniques for battling with unscrupulous credit bureaus, greedy creditors, and menacing bill collectors, this book teaches you how to break out of the system altogether in just a few easy steps. Not a rehash of old information, *Super Privacy* contains the latest inside information from the top professionals in the fields of personal finance, asset protection, and consumer law.

This book is for anyone who is tired of struggling to survive in an unfree system. It is for anyone who wants to start their life over again, free of the remnants of the past. It is for the millions of consumers who have had the misfortune of going through bankruptcy, divorce, a serious illness, a death in the family, or unemployment.

Super Privacy reveals inside information that "Big Brother" and the bureaucrats don't want you to know. It describes the government's recent attempts to thwart the efforts of new identity seekers through vital statistics cross-referencing and new technology. It even includes several ways to change your Social Security number, including how to have it changed officially by the Social Security Administration.

Armed with the information in this book, you will be able to circumvent the immense web of identification information systems and create another file (or files) overnight. Many consultants are charging clients as much as $3,000 to help set up new identification files. Now you can join the insiders who are privileged to have this powerful information at their disposal.

In the following pages you will learn essential information to help you survive and succeed in these uncertain economic times. You will learn how to:

- structure your property ownership to reduce your vulnerability to lawsuits, creditors, and asset forfeiture
- protect your cash holdings from confiscation, currency recalls, or other "monetary reforms"
- protect yourself from the government's new encoded currency that will be used to trace every cash transaction
- obtain government issued identification documents, including a driver's license, Social Security card, and passport
- set up offshore bank accounts and private trusts

Finally, you will learn exactly how to legally create a new identity and break free from the system once and for all. *Super Privacy* will help you start over in life and be the person you always imagined you could be, or perhaps were afraid to imagine. Even if beginning a totally new life is not your immediate goal, the knowledge you are about to receive will help you protect your privacy and financial assets.

Introduction

Stephen J. Shaw owed more than $100,000 to companies he'd never heard of.

His ordeal began when Steven M. Shaw, who sold used cars in Orlando, Florida, tapped into a computer at the auto dealership to look up credit files on his namesakes around the country. Rifling through dozens of electronic reports, Shaw browsed for clean records—files on people with lots of credit available and no delinquent accounts. His plan was to pose as people with pristine credit histories.

He obtained duplicates of his victim's credit cards and opened accounts at retailers and even took out car loans in their names—debts he never intended to repay. Then Shaw ran the credit checks again to make sure he wasn't pushing the capacity of his host's accounts too far.

Because Stephen J. Shaw, a 40-year-old Washington, D.C.-based free-lance writer, paid his bills on time and wasn't overextended financially, he became one of Steven M.'s victims. Unfortunately, by the time Stephen J. learned he was being robbed—thanks to an eagle-eyed loan processor at a credit union—his address had been changed to one in Florida (where he'd never lived), and he owed more than $100,000 to companies he had never heard of.

Eventually, Steven M. was convicted of bank and credit fraud and sentenced to 37 months in federal prison. Stephen J., in the meantime, has spent the last few years repairing his damaged credit rating and publicizing his plight at congressional hearings and on such talk shows as *Geraldo*, hoping to warn others before it happens to them.

Shaw has become something of a poster child for victims of data shakedowns, but his case is far from unique. What he's going through illustrates a dispiriting truth about privacy in the information age: it barely exists.

As more and more confidential records are posted on far-flung computer networks—accessible to everyone from home computer owners to real estate agents, insurance brokers, employers, private investigators, car salespeople, and marketers—no data is safe from prying eyes. Medical files, financial and personnel records, Social Security numbers, and telephone call histories—as well as information about our lifestyle preferences, where we shop, and even what car we drive—are available quickly and cheaply.

Ivy James Lay, a former MCI maintenance worker, used a small computerlike device to monitor calls as they surged through routing equipment and retrieve numbers that long-distance customers had typed on their telephone keypads. Then Lay (also known by his hacker name, Knight Shadow) browsed this data, isolated credit card numbers and PINs, and sold them. His customers used the numbers to play games and chat via computer. In all, MCI, AT&T, and four other phone companies lost nearly $50 million.

Lay's case is unusual for one reason—he was caught. Although theft of information from corporate computer and telecommunications systems continues to soar, few of the criminals are ever apprehended—mostly because the victimized companies would rather not publicize to shareholders, customers, and would-be thieves that they are vulnerable. Still, keeping quiet doesn't hide a disturbing fact of life in the corporate United States: protecting sensitive data and safeguarding networks are low priorities.

The accounting firm of Ernst and Young surveyed 1,271 companies and found that more than half had experienced computer-related break-ins during the past two years; 17 respondents had losses in excess of $1 million. And with more and more firms using the Internet, the Computer Emergency Response Team at Carnegie Mellon University reported nearly 4,000 hacking incidents last year, almost three times as many as the year before.

According to a former computer security chief at the National Security Agency (NSA), a Federal Bureau of Investigation (FBI) report details 400 open cases of computer-related espionage against U.S. businesses by foreign countries.

The Federal Trade Commission receives more complaints about credit reporting abuses than all other consumer issues combined. Inaccurate credit reporting costs consumers approximately $50 billion each year. The problem is that for data collectors, there's no profit in satisfying the public's demand for accuracy, just in selling information, which leaves consumers in a difficult spot: information providers have no incentive to protect data—whether accurate or erroneous—from landing in the wrong hands, and individuals have little recourse if it does.

Marketing companies compile lists of Americans based on their tastes, purchasing choices, and financial condition, as well as their age and physical characteristics. These companies can buy motor vehicle records from your state to get your address, date of birth, height and weight, and the type of car you drive. They can get change-of-address information from the U.S. Postal Service to determine who just moved and might be interested in furniture, carpets, and home equity loans. From credit bureaus, they can buy names of deadbeats (for marketing secured credit card offers and bankruptcy pitches). Supermarkets tell marketers what customers are buying based on information scanned at the checkout counter. And with caller ID systems, marketers can grab phone numbers of people who dial 800 and 900 numbers to identify who's in the market for a vacuum cleaner, an astrology magazine, or even pornography.

According to an investigation by the *Providence Journal Bulletin* in Rhode Island, for example, more than 50,000 telephone customers who paid to block their phone numbers from being read by caller ID systems never got that protection. This came to light only when a woman staying at The Shelter, a hideout for battered women in Alabama, dialed a friend in New England. She was stunned when her friend mentioned that he could see her phone number on his caller ID machine.

Employers Information Service (EIS) is a Gretna, Louisiana, information provider that has upwards of a million files on people whose only derogatory mark is that they had applied for worker's compensation. EIS subscribers—companies in the accident-prone oil, gas, and construction industries—tap the company's database when considering a prospective employee for a job. Filing for worker's compensation is not a crime, but if EIS has a record on a job applicant, they probably won't get the job.

After 15 years of supplying offshore rigs for Penzoil, Ernest Trent injured his arm permanently during a storm. Soon after getting worker's comp, the Bossier City, Louisiana, father of nine began looking for less strenuous work. He applied for 200 jobs and was turned down for all of them, despite a spotless work record.

EIS admits that its data has a hand in Trent's type of problem, but it argues that its purpose is to provide objective information, not make it impossible for worker's compensation claimants to find work.

The unfortunate reality of the matter is that computerized data is often viewed as implicitly accurate and conclusive, not as just another set of facts among many to consider when making a judgment about somebody.

Another perhaps even more frightening example of privacy invasion is the increasingly easy access people have to medical records. When U.S. Representative Nydia Velasquez first ran for office in 1992, her hospital records, detailing an attempted suicide the year before, were downloaded and faxed to newspapers and TV stations. Winning the election didn't dull the pain of this invasion of her privacy, says Velasquez. "I had no power to stop it. I felt violated."

So did victims of a scam perpetrated recently by a 13-year-old girl in Jacksonville, Florida. This daughter of a hospital clerk used her mother's computer to access hospital records. She then culled a list of emergency room patients and called seven of them to say they had tested positive for HIV, the virus that causes AIDS. She was charged with taking confidential data from computers and making threats.

These incidents become especially disturbing when you consider the Clinton administration's 1993 call for a universal health care program, which included a national network of patient records. Though the plan has been shelved for now, the idea of a nationwide data bank is still being championed by medical and insurance company lobbyists who support computerized cradle-to-grave medical files for every American.

A smaller version of this network is already in place. The data bank is run by Medical Information Bureau (MIB), is funded by nearly 100 insurance companies, and contains files that summarize the health conditions of millions of Americans. Insurers feed into the system whatever they learn from insurance applications, physician's files, and hospital records. Then MIB employees enter numeric codes for each condition. MIB even has codes for what the company considers habits of unhealthy lifestyles, such as skydiving, poor driving, sexual deviation, and an unkempt appearance.

This can lead to damaging errors. A New York writer applied for a life insurance policy with New England Life a few years ago. The next day he received a call from his insurance agent, very upset. The agent asked him, "Why the hell didn't ne you were being treated for extreme psychosis?"

had been wrong. Whoever typed his record into the database had tried to enter the code for mild anxiety—a condition the writer once saw a psychiatrist for—but the person had mistyped one number. It took the writer over a year to convince MIB to clean up his file, during which time no insurance company would cover him.

MIB admits that errors like this happen, but claims they don't occur often enough to outweigh the pluses the medical data bank provides.

In most cases, insurers will inform applicants that an MIB report contains derogatory information. Potential employers, on the other hand, are not so forthcoming when they find adverse information during a medical background check on a job applicant. If something disturbing shows up, applicants are rarely informed; they're just told they didn't get the job.

Government intrusion into our personal and financial lives is on the rise. Following the arrest of alleged terrorist Timothy McVeigh, President Bill Clinton submitted a bill to Congress that would, among other things, make it easier for federal authorities to check your personal records and to use electronic surveillance and wiretaps more freely. The proposed bill, H.R. 1710, would allow the government to secretly obtain your financial records without accusing you of any crime. H.R. 1710 would also allow the government to tap your phone and fax machine and secretly obtain your hotel/motel bills, vehicle rental records, public storage records, and your shipping invoices even though nobody, not even the government, thinks that you are guilty of any crime.

Just as frightening is Emergency Banking Regulation Number 1. This well-guarded secret was signed by Robert B. Anderson in 1966, who was President Dwight D. Eisenhower's secretary of the treasury in the previous decade. Emergency Banking Regulation Number 1 allows the president to freeze all bank withdrawals, checking account transactions, credit card transfers, and other attempts to use your own money, without congressional approval.

Other emergency powers allow the president to:

- control or prohibit all CB radio transmissions
- confiscate "excess property" owned by private citizens
- ration virtually the entire output of American industry
- shut down every private school in the country and take possession of the buildings for government use

There's no federal legislation safeguarding medical, telephone, employment, insurance, and bank records, and the two main privacy laws on the books—the Fair Credit Reporting Act (1970) and the Privacy Act of 1974—are toothless vestiges of the precomputer age.

Even the most secure government records aren't necessarily safe anymore, as some 60,000 users of Intuit's MacInTax tax preparation software found out this year. Intuit disclosed in March that a programming instruction that should have been deleted from the final code provided a way for Mac users to access others' electronically filed returns. "It's possible that anyone could have looked at someone's data or perhaps deleted a file," admits Mark Goines, vice president for Intuit's personal tax group.

The Internal Revenue Service (IRS) refuses to discuss the incident, claiming it can't vouch for the quality control procedures used by the companies involved in the IRS's electronic filing program—a remarkable concession considering that the confidentiality of tax returns is strictly protected by the Privacy Act of 1974 and the IRS code.

The IRS's response becomes less surprising, though, in light of the agency's own information scandal last year, which "confirmed the worst fears about government mismanagement of data concerning private citizens," says Arkansas Senator David Pryor (D).

In the midst of a $23 billion IRS computer-modernization campaign aimed at giving employees on-line access to taxpayer information, hundreds of IRS staffers were caught browsing through tax records of friends, neighbors, relatives, and celebrities, as well as altering files to create false returns.

As the paperless, cashless society approaches, information is becoming a hot commodity. That's why many state and local governments now sell, via computer, any information they have. Buyers can download drivers' files, home ownership records, and police and courthouse activity logs. This information, as confidential as some of it may seem, has always been public record and thus accessible. But before it was available through a PC, it was difficult to get and even harder to get anonymously. In the past, an investigator or skip-tracer had to go to separate state and local offices to request the information and then fill out numerous forms, which left an audit trail, before a clerk would agree to pull a file from an overstuffed cabinet.

Now, to ensure the widest possible market for their data and to avoid the problems associated with maintaining computer data bases, state and local agencies usually distribute this sensitive data through information brokers, eliminating nearly all of the previous safeguards on confidentiality.

For $10 to $20 per search, companies like CDB/Infotek, the National Credit Information Network, and U.S. Datalink offer an enticing cross-section of information. Now anyone can obtain information like how much the neighbors paid for their home, who holds their mortgage, their police records, where their assets are hidden, and who has sued them for bad debts. You can also purchase credit reports, Social Security numbers, and unlisted phone numbers (if you take down the person's license plate number).

In addition, there is also an underground network of information brokers who can obtain even the most sensitive data. One brochure lists bank account files for $200, credit charges for $150, post office boxes for $100, social security earnings for $150, safe-deposit box contents for $200, phone call logs for $200, and IRS records for $550.

In the following chapters you will learn more about possible intrusions into your personal and financial privacy and how to protect yourself. You will learn how to fight back and win against an unfair system and even turn it around to your advantage. By the time you finish this book, you will be among an elite group of insiders who have mastered the system and are now able to teach others. Most importantly, you will have the peace of mind and security of knowing that you are in control of your financial world.

CHAPTER ONE

American Dream— or Nightmare?

"Life, liberty, and the pursuit of happiness," are essential to the fabric of the American Dream. But what happened to that dream and the ideals from which it was conceived?

During the last decade, the U.S. government has enacted legislation that virtually nullifies the Constitution and the Bill of Rights. Consider the following charges by a citizens' rights organization:

- One in four families will be sued.
- Credit fraud and identification theft are among the fastest growing new crimes.
- Despite numerous lawsuits, fines, and proposed legislation,

Federal Trade Commission continues to receive more
nplaints related to credit reporting abuses than all other
problems combined.

- More than 30 million people are in trouble with the IRS.
- As the information superhighway continues to become a
  pervasive reality, concerns about privacy are increasing.
- Children older than one year must be identified on tax
  returns by their Social Security number.
- A passport application must contain your Social Security
  number. All passport applications are forwarded to the IRS.
- The IRS can compare your tax returns with credit bureau
  reports, U.S. Census data, county tax assessor files, and
  Department of Motor Vehicle records in order to determine
  whether you are overestimating your deductions or trying to
  hide assets from federal tax collectors.

INVASION OF THE ASSET SNATCHERS

In October of 1992, Donald Scott was awakened by the
sound of his front door being battered down and a cry for help
from his wife. Instinctively, he grabbed his handgun and hur-
ried downstairs, ready to defend his home and family. An
armed intruder ordered Scott to drop his weapon. He obeyed
the gunman's orders as the gunman put two rounds into the
center of Scott's chest, killing him instantly.

Scott's killers were specially trained agents from five separate state, county, and federal agencies—members of a secret
task force. Asset forfeiture was their specialty. They claimed to
have received a tip that Scott was growing marijuana on his
200-acre estate. The search was fruitless. No marijuana or drugs
of any kind were found. No charges were ever filed against Scott
or his wife.

It is widely believed by many in the community that local
bureaucrats wanted Scott's property, which bordered National
Park Service land, and that the search was designed to justify the
government's takeover of the adjacent property. Under civil asset
forfeiture statutes, the mere allegation that the property was being

used for some illegal activity, even without the owner's knowledge, would be sufficient cause for the property's forfeiture. The gunman who murdered Scott was never brought to trial.

According to a 1995 congressional report, government seizures have increased by 2,000 percent since 1985. Yet, according to the *Pittsburgh Press*, 80 percent of those who have had their property seized were never charged with any crime.

Any property-owning U.S. citizen, and any investor with property located in the United States, must become knowledgeable about the threat of civil asset forfeiture—the government's police power to confiscate your real and personal property based on that property's alleged use or involvement in criminal activities. The threat of government confiscation applies to homeowners; landlords; people with resort condos; investors; or partners in hotels, restaurants, and bars; and those who own farm or undeveloped land. Even retail business and commercial property owners are at serious risk.

Before dismissing the threat of asset forfeiture as a concern only of drug-related or money-laundering criminals, you should know that there are now more than 100 different federal forfeiture statutes addressing a wide range of illegal conduct, both criminal and civil. For instance, a woman had her automobile confiscated after police arrested her husband in the car with a prostitute. Talk about adding insult to injury!

In March 1996, attorney F. Lee Bailey was sentenced to six months in jail for refusing to turn over his $25 million fee to authorities. The government alleged that Bailey's client, a convicted drug dealer, had obtained the money through illegal activities, thus making his attorney's fees subject to forfeiture. While this may not garner most people's sympathy, imagine if the government wanted to confiscate your property because they said the money had passed through a drug dealer's hands.

In another case, a man who accepted five dollars from a friend for a ride was sentenced to a 10-year prison term. It turned out he was driving his passenger to a drug deal. By accepting money for the ride, the driver became a co-conspirator and thus was subject to a mandatory prison term.

If your car is stolen, it has by definition been used for an illegal purpose. Under the forfeiture laws in a number of states, this makes it forfeitable. I'm not aware of any forfeitures from car theft victims under this theory, but it's something to keep in mind, particularly if you live in a state like New Jersey, which permits forfeiture for "any indictable offense" connected with property.

New Jersey has one of the most severe forfeiture laws, which can be triggered by any alleged criminal conduct, even shoplifting! This statute denies the right to a trial by jury on the issue of forfeiture. In one case, a male gynecologist, Owen A. Chang, M.D., had his office equipment and building confiscated for being accused of conducting a medical exam on a female patient without the presence of a nurse, as required by local law. In another instance, Kathy Schrama watched local police seize her home, two cars, and all her furniture—even the Christmas presents she had purchased for her 10-year-old son—for being accused of stealing a UPS package from her neighbor's doorstep. A building contractor had his entire business confiscated by the state based on an allegation that his company made a construction bid for which it was not qualified.

Many states, including Texas, New Jersey, and Florida, apply civil forfeiture to any criminal activity, which means owners must police their real property against all criminal activity or possibly lose it. Homeowners and landlords are being forced not only into the role of their brother's keeper, but into being responsible for the acts of their children, spouses, guests, and tenants, even their tenant's guests.

In 1989, Congress made it a criminal offense to give false information on a loan application. The government is now using this law to confiscate the property financed with loan proceeds, even years later and even if all payments are up to date. In 1991, U.S. Marshals seized $11 million worth of commercial property, including five convenience stores, a multiplex movie theater, and a consumer electronics store.

In 1993, a federal circuit court ruled that defendants charged with illegally modifying, selling, and using television signal descramblers were guilty of federal wiretapping laws. Such acts are not only felonies, but forfeitable crimes, meaning your house could be seized if you install an illegal TV signal descrambler.

If this doesn't sound frightening, suppose it happens to you. Imagine facing a squad of armed forfeiture agents at your front door, or having your bank inform you that all of your accounts have been frozen.

Fortunately, it's not too late to fight back. By using perfectly legal techniques, you can make it nearly impossible for anyone to find out what you own or where you keep it!

"The only freedom which deserves the name is that of pursuing our own good, in our own way, so long as we do not attempt to deprive others of theirs, or impede their efforts to obtain it."

—John Stuart Mill

LEGAL REMEDIES

The word "privacy" never appears in the Constitution. It is only in the last century that this word has been used as a legal concept to describe the state's duty to leave people alone. A 1989 article by Louis D. Brandeis and Samuel D. Warren called "The Right to Privacy" helped arouse interest. In *Olmstead v. United States* in 1928, then Supreme Court Justice Brandeis said in his dissenting opinion, "The right to be let alone is the most comprehensive of rights and the right most valued by civilized men."

The primary safeguard for privacy in the U.S. Constitution is the Fourth Amendment. It asserts, "The right of the people to be secure in their persons, houses, papers, and effects, against unreasonable searches and seizures shall not be violated."

The First Amendment's guarantees of freedom of expression and assembly apply to the collection of data on political views and associations. Under the First Amendment's provision of free speech, individuals also have the right to say or not to say anything that doesn't directly harm or violate the rights of others. This includes the right to use whatever name and identifying information a person so chooses.

The Fifth Amendment's guarantee of due process of law

encompasses the presumption of innocence. Several court decisions have blocked the dissemination of arrest records not followed by convictions based on the presumption of innocence.

The Ninth Amendment has also been used as a protection of privacy. It asserts, "The enumeration in this Constitution of certain rights, shall not be construed to deny or disparage others retained by the people." According to Justice Brandeis, the Ninth Amendment guarantees in broader terms such rights as privacy emanating "from the totality of the constitutional scheme under which we live."

The Fair Credit Reporting Act of 1970 bars credit bureaus from sharing credit information with anyone but authorized subscribers. It gives consumers the right to review their credit records and be notified of credit investigations for insurance and employment. But the law allows credit agencies to share information with anyone it reasonably believes has a "legitimate business need."

In 1974, the Privacy Act was enacted to bar federal agencies from letting information they collect for one purpose be used for a different purpose. The law's exceptions, however, let agencies share data anyway.

Then there's the Right to Financial Privacy Act of 1978. It forbids the government from rummaging through bank account records without following set procedures, but it excludes state agencies, including law enforcement officials, as well as private employers. And more exceptions are tacked on every year. According to John Byrne, the federal legislative counsel for the American Bankers Association, "There's not a lot to this act anymore."

In 1987, a Washington, D.C., weekly, *The City Paper*, published a list of videotape titles borrowed by Robert H. Bork, then the U.S. Supreme Court nominee. As a result, Congress passed the Video Privacy Protection Act of 1988. Also known as the Bork Bill, it prevents retailers from selling or disclosing video rental records without a customer's permission or a court order. Too bad criminal, medical, insurance, and other records don't have the same protection.

Freedom of Information Act

Enacted by Congress in 1966, the Freedom of Information Act (FOIA) is based on the belief that government records should be open to the people. Before enactment of the act, individuals occasionally had to prove their right to look at government records. The FOIA shifted the burden of proof from the citizen to government; you no longer have to prove your need to see government records. Now, by law, you have the right to access them—unless the government can prove that the records you wish to see are "exempt" by law from that right.

The FOIA applies only to records of the executive branch of the federal government, not to those of Congress or the federal courts. Nor does it apply to records of any state or local government, or any private entity.

There are nine exemptions to the act, or reasons an agency can withhold records from the public. They cover (1) classified defense and foreign relations information, (2) internal agency personnel rules and practices, (3) material exempted by another statute from disclosure, (4) trade secrets and other confidential business information, (5) certain interagency or intraagency communications, (6) personnel, medical, and other files involving personal privacy, (7) investigatory records compiled for law enforcement purposes, (8) matters relating to the supervision of financial institutions, and (9) geological information on oil wells.

Although not required to do so, agencies often voluntarily release information that falls under an exemption unless they believe that disclosure is likely to cause harm. Interpretation of the act has raised many complex questions and disputes. Ultimately, the courts decide whether an agency is properly withholding records under an exemption of the FOIA.

Under the FOIA, you may request and receive any record that is in federal files and not covered by one of the exemptions. For example, suppose you have heard that a certain toy is being investigated as a safety hazard and want to know the details. In this case, the Consumer Product Safety Commission could probably help you. Or perhaps you want to read the latest inspection report on conditions at a nursing home certified for Medicare. Your local Social Security office keeps these records on file. You might want to know if the Federal Bureau of Investigation has a file on you. In all these examples, you may use the FOIA to request information from the appropriate federal agency.

When you make an FOIA request, you must describe the material you want. If the agency cannot identify what you've requested with a reasonable amount of effort, it is under no obligation to you. It is not required to do research for you or to compile or analyze data.

Although the FOIA does not apply to records of state or local governments, nearly all state governments have their own FOIAs. You may request information about a state's act by writing the attorney general of the state.

Although FOIA does not cover private business records, many private firms submit reports and other information to federal agencies. This is often necessary to do business with the government, to receive subsidies or licenses, or to engage in certain activities. Agencies usually withhold confidential commercial material that is contained in such reports. However, if the private firm has no objections, most agencies will provide such material to you. In addition, federal agencies may release some information from business firms even if the firm objects, i.e., if the information cannot be legally withheld. The FOIA does not require a private firm to release any information or records directly to you.

In contacting the federal government, each request for information must be made to the appropriate agency. For example, if you want information about a work-related accident at a nearby job site or manufacturing plant, write to the Department of Labor at the office in the region where the accident occurred. Or, if you want to know what your criminal record looks like, contact the FBI. Some of the larger departments and agencies have several Freedom of Information Offices. Some have one for each major bureau or other component; others have one for each region of the country.

You may have to do a little research to find the proper office to handle your inquiry, but you will save time in the long run if you send your request directly to the appropriate office. For assistance you can contact the nearest Federal Information Center (FIC). Located throughout the country, FICs are specially prepared to help you find the right agency, the right office, and the right address. These centers are operated by the General Services Administration. A booklet called the *Consumer's Resource Handbook* tells what federal agencies are responsible for specific consumer problems and where to write for assistance. The *U.S. Government Manual,* the official handbook of the federal government, may also be useful. It describes the programs within each federal agency and lists the names of top personnel and agency addresses. Both are available at most public libraries or can be purchased from the Superintendent of Documents.

When you get the agency's name and address, write a letter of request to the agency's Freedom of Information Office. Note on the envelope and at the top of the letter "Freedom of Information Request." Identify the records you want as accurately as possible. Although you do not have to give the document's name or title, your request must reasonably describe the records sought. Any facts or clues that you can furnish about the time, place, persons, events, subjects, or other details of the information or records you seek will be helpful to agency personnel in deciding where to search and in determining which records pertain to your request. This may save you and the government time and money and also improve your prospects of getting what you want.

A sample request letter is shown on page 18. Keep a copy of your request. You may need it in the event of an appeal or if your original request is not answered.

If you are not sure whether the information you want falls under one of the nine exemptions, you may request it anyway. It might help your case to state your reasons for such a request, even though the FOIA does not require you to do so. Agencies usually have discretion to release material that falls under these exemptions. Stating your reasons for a request may persuade an agency to give you access to records they might otherwise deny

Date

Agency Head or FOIA Officer
Name of Agency or Agency Component
Address

Dear_____ :

Under the Freedom of Information Act, 5 U.S.C. 552, I am requesting access to or copies of (identify the records as clearly as possible).

If there are any fees for copying or searching for the records, please let me know before you fill my request. (Or, please supply the records without first informing me of the cost if the fees do not exceed $_____.)

(Optional) I am requesting this information because (state the reason if you think it will help you obtain the information).

If you deny all or any part of this request, please cite the specific exemption you think justifies your refusal to release the information and notify me of appeal procedures available under the law.

(Optional) If you have any questions about handling this request, you may telephone me at _____ (home phone) or at _____ (office phone).

Sincerely,

Name
Address

Example Freedom of Information Act Request

as legally exempt. In addition, giving reasons for a request may help the agency locate information that is useful to you.

An agency may charge only for the cost of searching for the material and copying it. Searching fees usually run from $4 to $10 per hour; the rates generally reflect salary levels of the personnel needed for the search. The charge for copying letter-size and legal-size pages can run up to 35 cents a piece, but 10 cents per page is common in most agencies. If you wish to avoid copying charges, you may request to visit the agency in person to see the records.

Some agencies waive charges if the total cost is minimal. You may receive a waiver or reduction in fees if you request it and can show the information you are seeking will, when released, primarily benefit the general public. There is no requirement for uniform fees among the agencies.

Federal agencies are required to answer your request for information within 10 working days of receipt (excluding Saturdays, Sundays, and holidays). If you have not received a reply by the end of that time (be sure to allow for mailing time), write a follow-up letter or telephone the agency to ask about the delay.

Sometimes an agency may need more than 10 working days to find the records, examine them, possibly consult with other persons or agencies, and decide whether it will disclose the records requested. If so, the agency is required to inform you in writing before the deadline. They have the right to extend the deadline up to 10 more working days.

A few agencies sometimes receive unexpectedly large numbers of requests. If an agency has a backlog or requests that were received before yours, and it has assigned a reasonable portion of its staff to work on the backlog, the agency usually will handle requests on a first-come, first-served basis.

An agency normally will deny an FOIA request only if it has a serious practical problem with granting it, supported by a legal reason for denial (an exemption). If an agency denies your request, it must be able to prove that the information is covered by one of the nine exemptions listed in the act. The agency must give you the reason (exemption) for denial in writing and inform you of your right to appeal the decision.

Appealing A Denial

If your request for information is denied, you should promptly send a letter notifying the agency that you want to appeal. Most agencies require that appeals be made within 30 to 45 days after you get a notification of denial. The denial letter should tell you to whom your appeal letter should be addressed. Simply ask the agency to review your FOIA request and change its decision. It is a good idea to also give your reasons for believing the denial was wrong. Be sure you refer to all communications you have had on the matter. It will save time in acting on your appeal if you include copies of the original request for information and the agency's letter of denial.

The agency has 20 working days after it receives your appeal letter to respond. Under certain circumstances, it may take an extension of up to 10 working days. If, however, an agency took 10 extra days to deny your initial request, it would not be entitled to an extension on the appeal.

If you are willing to invest the time and money, you may take the case to court. You can file suit in the U.S. District Court where you live, where you have your principal place of business, where the documents are kept, or in the District of Columbia. The agency will have to prove that the withheld records, or the deleted parts of them, are covered by one of the exemptions listed in the act. If you win a substantial portion of your case, the court may require the government to pay court costs and reasonable attorneys' fees for you.

The Privacy Act

Closely related to the Freedom of Information Act is the Privacy Act, another federal law regarding government records. The Privacy Act gives individuals some control over how the federal government gathers, maintains, and disseminates personal information. The Privacy Act pertains only to records the federal government keeps on citizens and lawfully admitted resident aliens.

If you were ever in the military service or employed by a federal agency, there are records of your service. If you have ever applied for a federal grant or received a student loan certified by the government, there is a file. There are records on every individual who has ever paid income taxes or received a check from Social Security or Medicare.

The Privacy Act, passed by Congress in 1974, gives citizens some control over what personal information is collected by the federal government and how it is used. The act guarantees two basic rights: the right to see files about yourself, and the right to sue the government for permitting others to see your files without your permission or knowledge. Both of these rights are subject to a number of exceptions.

The Privacy Act only applies to documents about individuals maintained by agencies in the executive branch of the federal government. It applies to such records only if they are in a "system" of records, which means they can be retrieved by name, Social Security number, or other identifier. In other words, the act does not apply to information about individuals in records that are filed under other subjects, such as organizations or events, unless the agency routinely retrieves them by name, etc. Also, the act does not apply to records held by local governments or private organizations.

There are seven exemptions to the Privacy Act under which an agency can withhold certain kinds of information from you. Examples of exempt records are those containing highly sensitive information on national security or ongoing criminal investigations. Another exemption often used by agencies is that which protects information that would identify a confidential source. For example, if an investigator questions a person about your qualifications for federal employment and that person agrees to answer only if his identity is protected, then his name or any information that would identify him could be withheld.

The seven exemptions are listed in the act. If you are interested in more details, you may read the Privacy Act in its entirety. It is printed in both the *U.S. Government Manual* and the U.S. Code (Section 552a of Title 5), which are available in most public and school libraries. You may also order a copy of the Privacy

Act, Public Law 93-579, from the Superintendent of Documents, since it is too lengthy to publish as part of this book.

As with the FOIA, no single office handles all Privacy Act requests. To locate the proper agency to handle your request, follow the same guidelines as for the Freedom of Information Act.

The first step is to write a letter to the agency that has your file. Address your request to the Privacy Act Officer or head of the agency, such as "Secretary, Department of Health and Human Services." Be sure to write "Privacy Act Request" clearly on both the letter and the envelope.

Most agencies require some proof of identity before they will give you your records, so it is a good idea to enclose proof of identity (such as a copy of your driver's license) with your full name and address. Do not send the original documents. Remember to sign your request for information, since your signature is a form of identification. (A notarized signature is even better.) If an agency needs more proof of identity before releasing your files, it will let you know.

Under the Privacy Act, an agency can charge only for the cost of copying personal records about you, not for time spent locating them. You may avoid copying charges by requesting to visit the agency in person to see the records.

Under the terms of the Privacy Act, the agency is not required to reply to such a request within a given period of time, although some agencies have adopted time limits similar to the FOIA's 10-day response time, by regulation. If you do not receive any response within two weeks, write again, enclosing a copy of your original request.

If you think a particular agency has a file on you, you should write to the Privacy Act Officer or head of the agency. Agencies are generally required to inform you upon request whether they have files on you. In addition, agencies are required to report publicly the existence of all records systems they keep on individuals. The Office of the Federal Register annually compiles and publishes (or updates) a list of systems and any exemptions that apply to each. This multi-volume work, called the Privacy Act Issuances Compilation, is available at most large reference and university libraries or can be purchased from the Superintendent of Documents.

Most agencies require that you specify the systems of records you wish to have searched. If you do not know which systems to specify, give as much information as possible as to why you believe the agency has records about you. The agency should process your request or contact you for additional information.

The Privacy Act requires agencies that keep records containing personal information about individuals to maintain complete, accurate, and relevant files. If, after seeing your file, you believe facts are incorrect and should be amended, write to the agency official who released the record to you. Include any documentation that supports the changes you are requesting. The agency will let you know if further proof is needed. The act requires an agency to respond to such a request within 10 working days of receipt and to tell you precisely what will be done to amend the records. You may appeal any denial. Even if an agency also denies your appeal, you have the right to submit a statement explaining why you think the record is wrong. The agency will attach your statement to the record involved.

There is no standard procedure for Privacy Act appeals, but the agency should advise you of its own appeal procedure when it makes the denial. Should the agency deny your appeal, you may take the matter to court. If you win your case, you may be awarded attorneys' fees.

A Comparison of the Freedom of Information Act and the Privacy Act

Although the FOIA and the Privacy Act were enacted for different purposes, there is some similarity in their provisions. Both the FOIA and the Privacy Act give people the right of access to records held by agencies of the federal government. FOIA access rights are given to "any person," but Privacy Act access rights are only for the individual who is the subject of the records sought. FOIA applies to all records of federal agencies; the Privacy Act applies only to a majority of those federal agency records that contain information about individuals.

Each act has a somewhat different set of fees charged, time limits, and exemptions from its rights of access. If you request records about yourself, federal agencies may withhold them from you only to the extent that the records are exempt under both acts.

If the information you want concerns activities of federal agencies or another person, make your request under the FOIA, which covers all agency records. If the information you want is about yourself and you wish to avoid possible search fees, make the request under the Privacy Act, which covers most records of agencies that pertain to individuals. To maximize the chances of getting all the available information about yourself, getting it quickly, and with only a slight possibility of incurring a search fee, make the request under both acts. Sometimes you can use the FOIA to help you get records about yourself that are not in a Privacy Act "system." However, if the records you seek are covered only by the FOIA, you must be able to "reasonably describe" them, and you may be charged search fees. If you are in doubt about which act applies or would better suit your needs, you should probably base your request letter on both acts.

The FOIA contains one very important provision concerning privacy—Exemption 6. It may protect you from others seeking information about you, but it may block you if you seek information about others. FOIA Exemption 6 permits an agency to withhold information about individuals if disclosing it would be a clearly unwarranted invasion of personal privacy. This includes, for example, most of the information in medical and personnel files.

Exemption 6 cannot be used to deny you access to information about yourself, only to deny you information about other persons. To be covered by Exemption 6, the information requested must be (a) about an identifiable individual, (b) an invasion of the individual's privacy if disclosed to others, and (c) "clearly unwarranted" to disclose. Release of information about an individual is considered an invasion of privacy if he could reasonably object because of its intimacy or its possible adverse effects upon himself or his family. But such information is not protected by Exemption 6 if the injury to the individual is counterbalanced by a public interest favoring the release. For example, home addresses are exempt from release for unspecified or random uses such as commercial solicitation, but they are not exempt from release to state income tax authorities or state law enforcement.

If you are seeking information about a federal employee's working status, an agency usually will disclose his or her name, grade, salary, job title, and permanent work location, but an agency will not usually disclose similar information about an employee of a private business. Even federal employees, however, receive some privacy protection. For example, if you want to see the details of an investigative report that led to an employee's demotion, an agency might decide that disclosure of these details is not justified on public interest grounds.

IDENTIFICATION SYSTEMS

Various methods of identification are being tested by the international banking community. The simplest one is the electronic debit card with its black magnetic strip and personal identification number (PIN). But because of the recent rise in electronic fund transfer fraud, including ATM thefts, banks are working on other means of identifying the user.

One of those means is the hand-scan machine. Tests are now being performed in which this scanning machine is being used. You place your hand on a plate. The scanning device memorizes every mark on the palm of your hand. Your palm print is then identified and verified instantly.

The hand-scan machine could soon replace your credit card. The machine can "read" your right hand and assign you a number. When you go to the bank, you punch in the number, press your hand against the machine, and it accesses your account.

Other high-tech identification systems include voiceprint analysis and retinal blood vessel patterns (an automated system using a special camera to obtain and match unique retinal patterns in the eye).

early as January 1971, the details of a plan to track human
was revealed in *Transactions on Aerospace and Electronics*
magazine. The computer specialist who developed this
human tracking device called it the "Crime Deterrent
Transponder System." It was developed by the National Security
Agency as part of the Pentagon's Peacefare Program.

The Crime Deterrent Transponder System is a system for
attaching miniature electronic devices to criminals and other
suspected citizens and keeping track of them by computer. The
transponder emits radio signals in response to electronic pulses
received. The plan is now in full operation as a response to over-
crowded jails.

Several versions of a multipurpose computerized ID card
are also already in use. In Singapore, every person over the age
of 15 carries such a card, which is tied into computerized data
banks and permits access to information ranging from police
records to school loans.

In the United States, the Bush administration's 1988 drug
bill called for a national ID card system for gun owners. The
Justice Department, IRS, and FBI have long advocated such
cards. Eventually, each card would include a holographically
produced photograph, your fingerprints, a retinal scan, a genet-
ic scan, and your Social Security number.

Another proposal for a national ID card came from former
foreign service officer William Ridge. He suggested outlawing
all cash, bills, and coins. To replace cash, Ridge proposed a fold-
able card the size of a dollar bill that would contain information on your bank balance, credit limits, medical records, passport, and driver's license. To guard against theft, the card would
contain both a thumbprint and a photograph. Every individual
transaction using the card would build an electronic trail lead-
ing back to the purchaser. Drug abuse and money laundering
would be wiped out, says Ridge. The underground economy
would cease to exist. Since every transaction would create its
own record, no one would dare do anything illegal.

A 1991 conference in Barcelona, Spain, brought together
members of the International Card Technology Institute.

Speakers advocated the use of a "world passport card," which would contain an identification number unique to each carrier, along with medical data useful in an emergency. It would also contain information about your income, debt, criminal record, and other information.

Since 1989, the Marin (California) Humane Society has been implanting every dog and cat adopted from its shelter with an Infopet microchip ID, a high-tech answer to the age-old problem of identifying your beloved pet. The microchip, about the size of an uncooked grain of rice, is encased in biomedical-grade glass. The chip is imprinted with a 10-digit alphanumeric code and is implanted by simple injection between the animal's shoulder blades. With the wave of a hand-held scanner, the chip is activated to transmit the code to a computer which provides the owner's name, address, phone number, and any relevant medical information.

In the first year and a half that Infopet began offering the service, 10,000 pets were microtagged in California, Oregon, Missouri, Massachusetts, Arizona, and Canada.

Taken a few steps further, this same technology could theoretically be used to create the ultimate personal identification system—the implanted microchip (enter Twilight Zone music).

CRIMINAL JUSTICE INFORMATION SYSTEMS

Criminal justice information systems are the target of those most concerned about invasion of privacy. Criticism is aimed at the types of information stored in the systems, the validity of the data, the necessity for the information, the dissemination of the material, and the eventual purging or retention of the information.

The FBI maintains three basic categories of records: identification records, investigative files, and the National Crime Information Center (NCIC).

When a person is arrested by local, state, or federal law enforcement agencies, fingerprints and arrest data are forwarded to the FBI, which uses this information to compile the person's identification record. Such arrest records (often called "rap sheets") may later be used in identifying suspects, in locating fugitives, and providing guidance in setting bail, sentencing, and probation matters.

Since 1973, any person can request a copy of his own identification record from the FBI. If he then questions the accuracy or the completeness of any entry in that arrest record, he can arrange for it to be amended by the law enforcement agency that furnished the data.

The investigative files contain the results of investigations into matters within the FBI's jurisdiction. These files are composed almost entirely of interviews with citizens, officials, and informants.

The third category of files maintained by the FBI is the NCIC, which is a computerized index of stolen property, wanted persons, and criminal histories. Typically, the NCIC works like this: a policeman spots a car that arouses his suspicions. He radios its license number to headquarters, which in turn feeds the number into a computer and learns from NCIC whether it has been stolen. The policeman will be told in minutes whether the car is stolen, even if it's in a state halfway across the country from where it was stolen.

In general, the records stored in NCIC are more accurate and more complete than those maintained in the FBI's much larger Identification Division, and they are less widely disseminated. But because of its more sophisticated computerization, NCIC has inspired far greater fears than the Identification Division, a manual system operating mostly through the U.S. mail.

Criminal Records

George ran away from home at 14. For the next few years he was on the run. Along the way, he was arrested and convicted for several minor offenses. At 22, in Denver, he was married to a girl with no record. She got a job with a poverty agency, and he was a gas station attendant. For five years they saved almost every penny they earned, then he applied to an oil company to buy a franchise for a gas station of his own. George's juvenile record turned up even though he had concealed it. The franchise application was rejected.

Paul was arrested in Brooklyn for possession of marijuana. The charge was dismissed and he moved to Boston. He applied for a license to drive a cab. A temporary license was issued, but a week later he was ordered to report to the Boston Police Department's Bureau of General Services. His license was being revoked. The reason: a routine check with the FBI had disclosed an "open" charge of possession of narcotics pending in New York. His protest that the charge had been dismissed did no good. A year later Paul received formal notice that his license had been revoked because he was "not a suitable person to be licensed."

Walter was a diabetic. One day in a Long Island grocery store he had a diabetic seizure. He grabbed something sweet to eat and, as a result, found himself under arrest. When the reasons for his "theft" became known, the charges were dropped. Since Walter was a teenager at the time of the incident, he later brought suit to have the record of his arrest destroyed. He lost. Although juvenile arrest and disposition records are made confidential by the laws of 23 states, they still circulate freely.

When Tom was a teenager, he was arrested and convicted of some minor offenses: petty larceny, disorderly conduct, and escaping arrest. His last conviction came when he was 20 years old. Ten years later he applied for work with the City of Niagara Falls as an assistant filter operator. The Niagara Falls Civil Service Commission barred Tom from taking the required exam. Because of his criminal record, they said, he did not meet the standards for civil service employees: "good moral character and habits and satisfactory reputation."

Conviction records are the most damaging records to a person's life. Unlike arrest records, which are merely allegations often entirely unfounded and, at the very least, unsubstantiated, conviction records result from proof of guilt beyond a reasonable doubt or, more often, admission of guilt. There is a strong legal argument rooted in the concept of due process of law that the dissemination of conviction records should be forbidden. Our laws provide fixed penalties for crimes. The maximum penalty for any crime should be that fixed in the criminal law and no more. Distribution of conviction records makes a penalty lifelong and violates due process.

Out of Control

Dale was a 19-year-old former Marine who was arrested for burglary by the Los Angeles police. Dale was taken to a precinct station, booked, and fingerprinted, but he was subsequently released because, according to the police, they were "unable to connect [Dale] with any felony or misdemeanor at this time." For almost a decade Dale attempted to have all records of the incident destroyed.

Despite the fact that the LAPD admitted that Dale was not involved in criminal activity, it took him nine years to get those records destroyed, and then only with the help of the federal courts. The problem was not only the reluctance of police to destroy even irrelevant records, but the fact that copies of the records had been distributed outside the Los Angeles Police Department. Dale learned that his records were maintained not only in Los Angeles and by state law enforcement officials but also by the FBI.

In the course of litigation, Dale and his attorneys established that criminal records maintained by local, state, and federal police were available to a variety of criminal justice and non-criminal justice agencies. They discovered that the Identification Division of the FBI, which maintained a copy of Dale's record, operated without formal rules and routinely made its files available to organizations outside the criminal justice community, ranging from the U.S. Civil Service Commission to state and local organizations such as bar admission committees and taxicab license boards, and some private employers. Judge Gerhard Gessell, the federal judge who heard Dale's case, described the record exchange system operated by the Identification Division as "out of effective control."

The fact that the Identification Division of the FBI maintains rap sheets on more than 20 million individuals, 70 percent of which do not indicate any court dispositions, and that half of the almost 30,000 daily requests to see these records made by non-criminal justice agencies for licensing or employment, are clear reasons for concern.

33 WAYS TO PROTECT YOUR PRIVACY

1. Stop using your bank account for sensitive purchases. Use your present account only for routine expenditures and deposits and request your bank manager warn you in advance of any third-party requests for your bank records.

2. Make sensitive purchases with money orders, cashiers checks, cash, or other confidential means. Be sure to keep a receipt of all such purchases for tax purposes.

3. Avoid credit card purchases as much as possible. Pay off your old balances and close unnecessary accounts.

4. Establish an alternate checking or savings account for cashing checks and purchasing money orders, cashier's checks, or traveler's checks.

5. Establish a business checking account using a fictitious name and use it to transact business of a sensitive nature.

6. Limit your use of check writing to routine purchases only.

7. Avoid giving your Social Security number for identification purposes unless required to do so by law.

8. Keep a supply of cash, gold bullion, and/or silver coins at home in a safe place for emergencies or other uses.

9. Open a safe deposit box and place in it some portion of your wealth for safekeeping. Insure the contents and keep a record of the contents in a separate place. The ownership of the box should be in the name of a company, corpora-

tion, or trust to preserve privacy of the contents and allow immediate access after death.

10. Send money abroad, either in person or by mail, in a discreet manner. Use this money for investments or emergency purposes. Select a country that maintains a strict policy of financial secrecy and has a fairly stable government.

11. Avoid giving financial details and personal information when making investments or opening brokerage accounts. Emphasize nonreportable investments, but keep strict private records of all transactions.

12. When dealing with investment advisors or brokers, insist on signing a contract specifying that all correspondence and conversations will be confidential and that no information will be given out to third parties.

13. Obtain an unlisted number. Eliminate your street address from the telephone directory and list only your initials or middle name.

14. Rent a post office box or mail drop to receive all or a portion of your mail.

15. Remove your name from mailing lists. Write to the Direct Mail Marketing Association, 11 W. 42nd St., P.O. Box 3861, New York, NY 10163-3861, to have your name removed from most mailing lists. To have your name removed from lists sold to credit grantors and marketers, contact the three major credit reporting companies as follows:

Experian—P.O. Box 8030, Layton, UT 84041-8030. Tel. (800) 682-7654.

Equifax Options—Marketing Decision Systems, P.O. Box 740123, Atlanta, GA 30374-0123. Tel. (800) 219-1251.

TransUnion—555 West Adams St., 8th Floor, Chicago, IL 60661. Tel. (800) 851-2674.

16. Check your credit reports from all three major bureaus to make sure information is accurate. Correct any errors. To find out how to obtain a copy of your report call: Experian (800) 682-7654; Equifax (800) 685-1111; TransUnion (800) 851-2674.

17. When borrowing, use sources that require the least amount of personal and financial information—executive loans by mail, overdraft accounts, or collateral loans.

18. Apply for a passport to give you flexibility to travel around the world.

19. If you incorporate, consider a Nevada corporation for anonymity and avoid going public if at all possible.

20. Set up a living trust through your attorney to preserve personal and financial privacy as well as avoid the costs of probate at the time of your death.

21. Keep a low profile. Take your name off the front of your house and your mailbox. Don't use personalized license plates. Avoid owning extravagant cars or homes.

22. Build hidden safes and secret storage facilities for your valuables.

23. Hire a tax attorney to maximize the confidentiality of your return.

24. Read the disclosure statements before you sign a credit application. Know how much privacy you're about to give up.

heck your Social Security records periodically to make
rtain no one else is using your number. (Call 1-800-
34-5772 to request a form.)

26. Use an assumed name in private correspondence. For even greater privacy, establish one or more alternate identities with complete documentation. Many people I know keep a set of alternate identity documents (birth certificate, driver's license, Social Security card) in a safe place in case of emergency. Send sensitive correspondence without a return address.

27. Ask your accountant and attorney to return any nonroutine documents in their possession relating to you.

28. Use pay phones for calls that you wish to keep private.

29. Set up trusts and limited partnerships to protect your assets from lawsuits or government seizures.

30. Continue to educate yourself about the system. Know your rights. Read books that will help you get out of debt, protect your assets, improve your credit rating, and become financially independent.

31. Start a low-overhead, high-profit business that can be operated out of your home in your spare time. Reinvest your profits into your business until you have a well-honed money machine that can take care of your family's financial needs.

32. Keep your mouth shut. Don't discuss private matters, especially regarding your finances, with casual acquaintances.

33. Secure the doors and windows of your home against intruders. Consider using an alarm system or countersurveillance equipment for your home, car, and business.

CHAPTER TWO

Survival Investing

As the cashless society approaches, it is essential to look at investing from a new perspective. Survival investing is a phrase that has been around for quite a while. It was popularized by people like Mark Skousen, Howard Ruff, Harry Browne, Doug Casey, and other "hard money" investors. The following is a summary of survival investment strategies designed to take you through the 21st century.

KNOWLEDGE IS POWER

As Benjamin Franklin so aptly said, "An investment in knowledge pays the best dividends." Invest in your education. Learn how the system works. Find new and creative ways to free yourself from the bondage of economic slavery. Begin by unshackling your mind from the chains of ignorance. Read the books listed in the back of this guide as a starting point in your journey along the road to economic enlightenment. Learn practical skills, such as computers, credit repair, auto mechanics, gardening, or a foreign language. As you continue to increase your knowledge base, your income opportunities will multiply as well. By learning how to structure your assets, for example, you can save thousands of dollars in taxes, legal fees, or possible forfeitures. Understanding the credit system can save you hundreds of thousands of dollars in interest payments, points, and finance charges. You can also learn how to make money by starting a small business from your home in your spare time, or you can learn a skill that can be developed into a second job.

DEBT IS SLAVERY

Get out debt. Pay off your bills. Negotiate with your creditors and settle your outstanding accounts. In the coming cashless society, becoming debt-free will be essential for survival and freedom.

Considering that the amount of interest you pay to your various creditors far exceeds the amount of interest you are probably receiving on savings accounts, certificates of deposit, and other investments, you would be wise to pay your debts off quickly and completely. Set a goal to become debt-free as soon as possible and develop a plan to put into immediate effect.

In the meantime, don't keep borrowing more money. Avoid using credit cards and overdraft checking accounts as much as possible. If you can't afford to pay cash for something, consider saving your money until you can. It will probably still be there, and the price may even have gone down.

Consider driving a less expensive vehicle, and if you own your home, talk to your bank about refinancing at a lower interest rate and accelerating your mortgage payments. One way to do this is through a bi-weekly plan. Mortgage acceleration plans can save you thousands of dollars in interest payments and allow you to pay off your home in up to half the time. For more information on mortgage reduction strategies, write Financial Dynamics, P.O. Box 51581, Riverside, CA 92517-2581.

TOOLS OF PRODUCTION

Whether you are a mechanic who uses wrenches, hammers, and drills, a writer who uses a word processor, paper, and pens, or a manufacturer who uses warehouses, presses, and lathes, the principle is the same. Tools of production create wealth. By purchasing tools and facilities now, rather than keeping your money in the bank, you will have the ability to increase your income. Paper wealth will decline in value, while your ability to produce wealth will increase.

By combining your tools with your increased knowledge, you can pay off your debts and free yourself from the system. You can also practice guerrilla capitalism to even further enhance your opportunities for success.

Stockpiling

You should also consider stockpiling the supplies, raw materials, and inventory required for your business. The carpenter who supplies his own nails and lumber will be at a distinctive advantage should there ever be a shortage of cash.

Precious Metals

Precious metals, particularly gold and silver, have been used as a medium of exchange for thousands of years. Throughout history currencies have come and gone, but gold and silver have remained. Many governments, including our own, have sought to restrict individual ownership of gold and silver. U.S. coins no longer have precious metals in their contents, and paper currency is no longer backed by a gold standard.

As the U.S. dollar declines in value, the price of gold and silver will go up. It is possible that precious metals will multiply in value during the next few years. It is also possible that the government may once again prohibit American citizens from owning "excessive quantities" of precious metals.

My advice is to put at least 10 percent of your investment assets into gold and silver coins and store them in a safe place. By making small purchases with cash, it will be difficult for Big Brother and the bureaucrats to trace your investments. It is also possible to move your precious metal assets out of the country without violating the law. This may change by the time this book goes to print, however, so act prudently in this regard.

Gold and silver coins can also be used for barter. As I will discuss in "The Beauty of Barter," this is one of the few remaining realms of free enterprise in the coming cashless society.

Consumables

What would you do if you went to the bank one day and all your accounts had been "frozen"? What if the stores refused to take your cash, your checks, or your credit cards? This is exactly what happened in Russia during a recent currency recall. It could happen here as well.

One of the best books I've ever read on the subject of investing in consumable supplies is John A. Pugsley's *The Alpha Strategy*. Here is a quote from the book to give you an idea of its premise:

> As long as you have your wealth in the form of paper claims, you are prey to swindlers and con men, both those who work through government and those who work outside the law. Since almost all of the manipulation, subterfuge, and theft of your wealth occurs while it is in paper claims, you have a simple and obvious defense; keep your wealth in real goods instead of paper claims. The only safe, rational investment program for the average person in today's turbulent economy is to eliminate the intermediate step. Instead of converting labor into money, money into investments, investments back into money, and money into real goods, simply stated, invest your savings in those real things that you will be consuming in the future. Save only real wealth.

Pugsley advises consumers to store up on nonperishable food items, water, cleaning supplies, personal items, and paper products. By purchasing these items in bulk, you can save money and avoid the possibility of future shortages.

A more radical approach to stockpiling consumable goods is offered by economist Gary North. In his book *Government by Emergency* he recommends stockpiling high-demand barter items such as cigarettes, liquor, coffee, and ammunition. North also recommends obtaining such items as shortwave and CB radios, survival kits, guns, and ammunition in order to prepare yourself for the inevitable "emergency" to come.

THE BEAUTY OF BARTER

A woman recently approached me and asked me if I could help her repair her credit rating. She told me that she had read my book *Life After Debt* after hearing me on the radio and she wanted some personal advice. She also mentioned that she was the publisher of an annual business directory that targeted minority and women-owned businesses.

I offered to take a look at her credit reports and give her a comprehensive evaluation along with specific recommendations and referrals.

"How much do you charge?" she asked.

"Don't worry about it," I replied. I then offered to provide her with a consultation in exchange for advertising space in her directory.

She received a complete evaluation of her credit reports, along with specific recommendations and referrals. I received a quarter-page ad for my book. It was a win-win situation without having to use money as a medium of exchange.

Such is the beauty of barter, the oldest and most direct method of doing business. Barter has been used for thousands of years before money and all its complications were ever invented.

Barter was used in early America to trade between the colonies and England. Many pioneers existed for years without ever seeing money. They paid their taxes and bought what they could not produce by bartering for it. Here are some of the many advantages of barter.

Conserving cash. Conserving cash is essential during these uncertain economic times. By trading for what you want you can hang on to your cash and still get what you need.

Giving both parties a better deal. People don't need money, they need things. Money is simply a middle step that often gets in the way of a clean transaction. When you barter for something you can afford to forego the "profit" you would have made on a sale because you are getting what you would have spent that profit on. In effect, both parties are getting what they want at wholesale.

Creating value. To the extent that you can trade something of lesser utility to you for something of greater utility, the item of lesser utility has value. In other words, even if something isn't worth anything else to you, it is valuable as trading material.

Increasing opportunities. By bartering your skills instead of just selling them you can increase your opportunities considerably. Even if your skill is not one that is in general demand, or if there are hundreds of others in your area with the same skill, you will increase your opportunities by offering to barter.

Building trading relations. If you're willing to barter for what you want, you'll find that you will build up steady relations with other barterers. This produces a valuable kind of customer loyalty.

Beating the bureaucrats. During the current administration we can expect price controls, wage controls, profit controls, and taxes, taxes, taxes! A barter exchange is much more difficult for bureaucrats to control than a sale. Many of the new regulations will ignore barter transactions. Those that don't are going to present headaches for the enforcers.

Karl Hess, an ex-liberal, ex-conservative, ex-urban homesteader who once was Barry Goldwater's speech writer, now lives in rural West Virginia. He is absolutely penniless. Nonetheless, he gets by. The IRS has a lien against his property for nonpayment of income taxes. In response, Hess has earned his living by bartering for a decade. He earns no money by design. He trades his sculptures for whatever he can get. He gets by. The IRS gets nothing.

By using barter you'll be able to avoid many of the problems inherent in the kind of increasing regulations we are sure to see in the coming cashless society. Barter is one of the purest forms of free enterprise available, which makes it essentially difficult for the bureaucratic mind to comprehend and control.

The bad news about barter is that the IRS considers the value you gain in barter as taxable income. The good news is that it's an easy regulation to promulgate and a hard one to enforce. Failure to report value gained in trades as income constitutes tax evasion and is a crime. Reporting a low value established by a written agreement is not a crime.

According to Dyanne Asimow Simon, author of *The Barter System*, "Barter is a form of individual guerrilla economics, spearheading autonomous attacks on middlemen, taxes, and the corporate squeeze. . . . Do not underestimate the power of the swap. It possesses all the advantages of traditional guerrilla tactics. It does not require large troops; it is flexible, hard to pin down, and once it's gone, it leaves no trace. It does not depend on fancy offices, elaborate equipment, or rigid schedules. It works as well in the city as it does in the woods."

To prepare for bartering, assess your skills and possessions. What do you have to trade? People need both goods and services. Your products and skills can be either something you do as an occupation or a hobby or second trade. Examples of products you could use for barter include:

- self-help books
- computers, hardware, tools, etc.
- foods grown in your backyard
- things you can make, such as furniture or sculpture
- stockpiled consumable goods

Examples of services you can use for barter include:

- financial consulting

- baby-sitting
- typing/word processing
- plumbing and electrical contracting
- tutoring
- medical care
- bookkeeping/accounting
- manual labor

How do you get started in bartering? Simple, just ask the other person if they'll trade for the item you want. In a surprising number of cases you'll find that you can come to a mutually agreeable arrangement. Because value in a barter deal is subjective, you'll discover that you can put together deals where both parties feel that they're giving less and getting more than they would in a cash arrangement.

CHAPTER THREE

Financial Privacy

Privacy has been a historically important issue. Many feel it is a basic right. There are many legitimate reasons why people want and deserve their privacy.

Achieving financial privacy can be an important factor in preventing unnecessary lawsuits. It can also help you protect your assets from government seizure. By structuring your assets in such a way that they are virtually untraceable, they become invulnerable to litigation, government seizure, or theft.

It is important to remember that in a government seizure, the burden of proof is on you to demonstrate by the preponderance of the evidence that your assets have been seized in error. On the other hand, if your assets are in a form that the government (or any other litigant) cannot attach prior to trial, you will be in a much stronger legal position.

It is also important to take action before you are subject to litigation. Any effort you make to protect your assets after litigation begins may be illegal under the fraudulent conveyance statutes. Technically, such actions could even be determined to constitute criminal offenses under racketeering or money laundering statutes.

MONEY LAUNDERING

The Commission on Organized Crime estimates that between $5 billion and $15 billion of the $50 billion to $75 billion in drug money earned annually in the United States is funnelled offshore. In addition to narcotics trafficking, substantial amounts of cash generated through a variety of nondrug crimes, such as illegal gambling, loan-sharking, and commercial fraud, also have to be "laundered."

In addition to actual shipments of cash, precious metals, and gemstones, money is also laundered through electronic funds transfer (EFT) systems. However, huge sums are also transferred electronically each year in connection with such conventional banking activities as collections, reimbursements, letters of credit, and foreign exchange transactions. In 1990, the Clearing House Interbank Payment System, the primary wholesale international electronic funds transfer system, processed about 37 million transfers between the United States and international banks valued at $222 billion.

Laundering large amounts of cash can pose considerable problems, given the sheer weight and bulk of currency. According to the Customs Service, U.S. currency notes weigh about 1 gram, with about 450 bills to the pound. Thus $227,000 in $10 bills weighs about 50 pounds. Money laundering has become an increasingly sophisticated and specialized business, often conducted by independent money-laundering experts who are usually working for a percentage of the laundered funds.

Enforcement efforts can target money laundering at different stages of the process.

Placement. This involves the physical disposal of bulk cash through various means, including commingling with legitimate business proceeds, smuggling, and converting cash into deposits or assets at banks. Launderers can also place cash through other financial institutions such as casinos, check-cashing establishments, currency exchanges, securities brokers, and nontraditional channels like underground banking systems that deal in barter.

Layering. This confuses and disguises the source and audit trail of dirty money by moving funds between accounts and transferring funds electronically.

Integration. This involves bringing the laundered funds back into the legitimate economy with the appearance of having been derived from legal sources. Real estate deals, loans through "front" companies, and false import/export invoicing are among the common integration techniques.

Money can be moved into international channels in an almost limitless number of ways. Physically smuggling currency and/or financial instruments out of the country is one of the primary laundering techniques, accounting for billions of dollars annually, according to the State Department. Launderers can use domestic banking institutions to move funds internationally by making direct or indirect cash deposits and having the bank wire these funds to an overseas account. Money can also be laundered internationally by purchasing commodities such as cars, appliances, or precious metals and shipping them abroad to be sold for local currency, or by falsely invoicing international commercial transactions. By overstating the value of exports, for example, a launderer can justify funds received from foreign sources. Finally, launderers increasingly rely on nonbank financial institutions as currency exchanges, including *casas de cambio,* small exchange houses often located along the U.S. border with Mexico.

PROTECTING YOUR PERSONAL ASSETS FROM JUDGMENTS

Can you imagine the following? You own a home-based

business. Everything's going fine until one day an employee has a fatal accident on the way to a business appointment. Or business slows down and you fall behind on payments to your suppliers.

You are sued and the judge rules against you. The attorneys for your opponent seize not only your business assets, but also your home, your car, your personal bank and savings account, and everything else of yours they can lay their hands on.

Nowadays, people don't care about who's right or wrong. Today, it's all about who has the money. Deep pockets. Asset searches can determine your ownership of bank accounts, vehicles, boats, businesses, real estate, and any other assets listed in your name.

One of the fastest, most efficient, and inexpensive methods of protecting yourself is by incorporating your business. For a nominal fee, you can have an incorporation service establish your business as a corporation.

A corporation is a unique "legal entity" with its own existence, taxes, and other liabilities. You are not the corporation, and the corporation is not you. As a separate legal entity, it can enter into contracts, hold title to property, open bank accounts, invest, sue, or be sued. This allows you to have the corporation enter into ventures with potential risk that you would rather not take upon yourself. A corporation can thus provide very valuable flexibility and privacy.

Insiders often refer to the corporation as "the ultimate tax shelter" for the excellent tax benefits it can provide. And unique protection of personal assets from the risks of corporate activity is available to the owners, officers, and directors.

LEGAL TAX AVOIDANCE

It is important to understand the difference between "tax avoidance," which is perfectly legal, and "tax evasion," which is illegal. Tax avoidance is simply avoiding situations which are taxed, while tax evasion is failing to pay taxes that are due.

Driving a few extra miles to cross a free bridge in order to avoid a nearby toll bridge is avoidance. Crossing the bridge without paying the toll would be evasion.

Avoiding burdensome taxes is wise and often necessary in order to protect yourself and to survive in today's business world. It is neither illegal nor immoral.

Forming a corporation in a tax-free state, such as Nevada or Wyoming, and arranging for the profits to accumulate there rather than in the high-tax state in which you may be doing business can minimize or eliminate your state taxes.

By setting up a corporate base in either Nevada or Wyoming, you can take advantage of these states' pro-business attitudes, while doing business anywhere in the world. Nevada's privacy, liability protection, and tax-free status for corporations have made it the clear choice as the preferred state for incorporation. Experts in the fields of asset protection, privacy, and tax strategies often refer to Nevada as America's "tax haven." Wyoming has enacted similar legislation, making it another attractive choice for incorporating.

Nevada has no state corporate taxes, no taxes on corporate shares, no franchise tax, no personal income tax, and is the only state with no information-sharing agreement with the IRS. Likewise, Wyoming has no franchise tax, corporate income tax, or tax on corporate shares and none of their accompanying reporting requirements.

Many business activities can be conducted through a Nevada or Wyoming corporation with substantial tax savings. The corporation may have investment income, rental income, dividend income, or royalty income. It may generate receivables, such as leases, or payments for goods or services. These and other business activities may be perfect for the proper, legal use of a Nevada or Wyoming corporation. By so doing, you may save substantial tax dollars.

Capital Asset Management is one of the best incorporation services I am aware of. The company deals with setting up Nevada and Wyoming corporations as well as limited liability companies (LLCs). Write Capital Asset Management, 41750 Winchester Road, Suite N, Temecula, CA 92590.

The Dual Corporation Strategy

If the nature of your business requires that your primary business activity be performed in a state with high corporate or business taxes, you can still take advantage of a separate Nevada or Wyoming corporation.

Simply divide your activities using a "dual corporation" strategy. The corporation or business in your home state still conducts business there, but other functions are performed by the tax-free corporation and are billed to the home state company. This strategy will work for any number of services or products that your company requires and is much easier and affordable than you might think.

For example, your business, like any company, needs to advertise to generate sales. Rather than providing this service in-house, suppose you form a Nevada or Wyoming corporation with which you can contract for these services to be provided.

Suppose your company spends $20,000 per year in advertising and generates $60,000 in annual taxable revenue in your home state. You form a Nevada or Wyoming corporation to provide the advertising services by negotiating the required contracts.

The Nevada or Wyoming corporation pays the $20,000 in hard costs and then bills the home-state business, say, $75,000 for services rendered. The tax-free corporation in Nevada or Wyoming has a profit margin for that year of $55,000. Your home-state business only shows $5,000 of net revenue. If the state corporate income tax rate in your home state is 9 percent, your tax-free corporation saved $4,950 in state corporate income taxes.

This type of interstate commerce is perfectly legal. You must, however, make sure the work provided by your Nevada or Wyoming corporation is actually performed. All products or services should be billed and invoiced accordingly.

This method of transferring income and profit from high-tax jurisdictions to low-tax jurisdictions is often called "upstreaming" or "transfer pricing," and it will work for many goods and services that your business already requires.

So, even if you are already incorporated or have a business in another state, a Nevada or Wyoming corporation can be an effective part of your tax planning strategy. It can be the competitive edge you have been looking for.

BECOMING JUDGMENT PROOF

The first thing an attorney will do when considering a lawsuit is run an asset search on all parties concerned in order to locate vehicles, real property, bank accounts, and investment holdings. However, if your property is owned by a corporation, then it may not be traceable to your name. Additionally, if your corporation has no assets, or the assets are completely secured, there is nothing to take. You become a less attractive target for a lawsuit.

Using the dual corporation strategy, let's assume that your home-state business asks your Nevada or Wyoming corporation for a loan. Your Nevada or Wyoming corporation agrees to lend $10,000, but demands an official lien, complete with the appropriate UCC-1 filings, against business assets to secure the note.

Your Nevada or Wyoming corporation will set the interest rates as high as necessary in order to become comfortable with the loan. If the home-state business doesn't make payments, compound interest will rapidly put the home-state business in debt to the Nevada or Wyoming corporation. If the interest is paid, it is a fully deductible business expense to your home state business, as well as income to your tax-free Nevada or Wyoming company.

Because all your major assets are now pledged to creditors, you suddenly have become a much less attractive target for a lawsuit. Even if an adversary won a judgment against you and closed your facility, your Nevada corporation would simply take possession of all those assets to which it is legally entitled.

Additionally, under Nevada and Wyoming law, corporate officers and directors are individually protected from liability for any action they might take on behalf of the corporation, which they had reason to believe was legal.

Note: Tax avoidance and judgment proofing should never be your primary purpose for using these strategies. Your primary purpose should be to achieve some business benefit. Tax savings and liability protection are incidental benefits of establishing your corporate base in Nevada or Wyoming. For assistance in setting up a corporation in Nevada or Wyoming, write: Financial Dynamics, P.O. Box 51581, Riverside, CA 92517-2581.

CORPORATE SHELL GAMES

Nevada and Wyoming corporation laws provide mechanisms for maintaining financial privacy.

First, stockholders are not public record. It is not possible to obtain a list of corporate stockholders from Nevada or Wyoming. They keep no such list. This means that ownership and control of a Nevada or Wyoming corporation can be nearly impossible to discover.

Nevada law provides a statutory barrier to anyone, including creditors, from gaining access to information on a corporation's stock ledger. Even another stockholder in the corporation may have no right to the stock ledger unless he owns more than 15 percent of this interest in the company.

The penalty in Nevada for using stockholder information for any purpose other than to have a stockholder defend or demonstrate his or her interest in the corporation is up to one year in jail and a $2,000 fine. Clearly, an individual who is not a stockholder in a Nevada corporation has no right to view or obtain the stock ledger.

Wyoming law specifically states that the right to inspect corporate records, including the stock ledger, is reserved for shareholders who have been on record for at least six months and who have at least 5 percent corporate ownership.

Bearer Shares

Nevada law also permits corporations to issue stock in the form best suited to guarantee an owner's anonymity: bearer shares. A stock certificate issued to "Bearer" may be redeemed by anyone who has it. That means the ownership is easily transferred. Additionally, the stockholders' names are not reflected in the corporation's records until such time as the shares are redeemed. Nevada is the only state that allows for this type of anonymous ownership.

The corporation's resident/registered agent keeps on file the name and address of the person who holds the stock ledger (the list of stockholders), but the resident agent is not required to keep the ledger itself. The stock ledger may be kept anywhere in the world. Used in this way, a Nevada or Wyoming corporation may be an invaluable tool for ensuring total financial privacy.

AGED CORPORATION SHELLS

In addition to setting up your own private Nevada or Wyoming corporation from scratch, it is also possible to obtain corporations that have been previously formed, but have never been used. These corporations have issued no stock and are guaranteed to have absolutely no debts, liabilities, or other encumbrances. They do, however, have federal taxpayer identification numbers.

An aged corporation shell can offer subtle yet significant advantages to you. If you do not have the luxury of time necessary to form a new corporation from scratch, you can purchase an aged shell in a matter of minutes. You can receive a complete corporation and corporate kit literally overnight by using a corporate service company or asset protection specialist.

An older corporation can also suggest prestige and credibility. As we all know, appearance and perception can count for a great deal in the business world. The name of the aged shell can be easily changed if you desire.

These aged corporations come with a name and a history of having paid the required state fees and can be used immediately.

OFFICE MANAGEMENT CONTRACTS

Any corporate strategy used to protect yourself from liability, make yourself judgment proof, enhance your financial privacy, or eliminate your state corporate taxes could be set aside if your corporation were not also a viable, operating business. The more you can demonstrate that the corporation is a viable, functioning business enterprise, the less likely it is that the corporation will be set aside as a "sham" (having form, but no substance).

A simple mailing address or post office box may give a false sense of security. Such a skeletal corporate presence will not stand up to the requirements of doing business. This is especially true as states are becoming increasingly aggressive and sophisticated in auditing interstate business activity.

By enlisting the services of a corporate service company you can obtain complete office management services, including answering service, fax lines, receptionist, conference rooms, photocopiers, printers, clerical support, and banking services. Most of these companies can also assist you in obtaining local and state business licenses, nominee officers, directors, and registered agents. The Directory of Consumer Credit Services contains a comprehensive listing of asset protection services and companies that specialize in setting up corporations. Corporate Service Center in Reno, Nevada, offers an excellent office management contract for a reasonable annual fee. Write: Corporate Service Center, 1280 Terminal Way, Reno, Nevada 89502.

LIMITED LIABILITY COMPANIES

The limited liability company is a new type of business entity that provides for the liability protection of a corporation and the flowthrough taxation of a partnership. An LLC is a unique entity that protects all of the owners and gives them the right to participate in management.

The owners are called "members" and can consist of individuals, partnerships, trusts, corporations, etc. Their liability is limited to their investment in the company. The LLC may have external management, or the members may manage the company directly.

The LLC is governed by individual state statutes. As a statutory entity, the LLC requires more formality in its development than an informal partnership.

The statutes that create the LLC contain the partnership characteristic of limited life. This means that, technically, it will dissolve upon the death, bankruptcy, or withdrawal of a member. But dissolution does not necessarily mean termination. The remaining members can decide to reorganize or take other appropriate action.

The LLC does not limit the number of owners as an S corporation does, nor does it restrict their type. An LLC can also allow for unlimited nonmember owners whose activities do not trigger events of dissolution.

However, the LLC is not allowed to have the corporate characteristic of free transferability of interests. A member may assign its right to income, but not the decision-making ability.

LLC Uses

The following list of LLC uses is provided to make you aware of some of its uses that you may not have considered.

Real estate. Liability protection, partnership tax treatment, and the ability of owners to be involved make a LLC a worthy alternative to joint ventures and limited or general partnerships.

Family businesses. The absence of S corporation restrictions makes the LLC a preferred entity in many general and family business ventures.

Professionals. The limited liability feature may save a professional from losing personal assets when his partner is in error.

Venture capital. A venture capitalist can exercise the control he desires and define situations that trigger sales rights. The LLC is particularly effective when investors are overseas.

Estate planning. Discounting valuations on gifts of minority interests are easier to justify when the interest consists only of economic interest without management participation.

Asset protection. Use of the LLC provides a better vehicle for those who desire protection from creditors, unhappy spouses, and business associates.

Immigration. The LLC allows aliens to attain their U.S. immigration goals with the protection of limited liability. (There are no citizenship requirements for members of a LLC.)

OTHER ASSET PROTECTION STRATEGIES

In addition to corporations and limited liability companies, there are several other strategies that can provide adequate protection from lawsuits, government snoops, asset forfeiture, or theft. The following is a brief list of some other asset protection strategies:

Irrevocable trusts. Irrevocable trusts have been recognized by virtually every U.S. court to be separate from the estate of the individual who established the trust. Assets held in a properly structured irrevocable trust cannot be seized to satisfy a judgment or seizure order.

A revocable trust, on the other hand, is one in which you maintain control over the trust assets and can terminate the existence of the trust at any time, withdraw assets, or change beneficiaries. These trusts provide very little, if any, asset protection.

One very powerful asset protection technique is to form a corporation and place the corporate stock into an irrevocable trust. For even greater protection, you could form several trusts. If one trust is seized, others would continue to protect at least a portion of your assets.

For even greater protection, you can have the trust established in a foreign country. This can get complicated, so be sure to get the help of an attorney or asset protection specialist.

Family limited partnerships. These structures can be used either by themselves or in combination with other structures. For example, you could form a corporation and transfer stock into one or more family limited partnerships. The corporation could serve as the general partner. The best way to do this is to appoint a corporate general partner not connected to you in any way. Your children, spouse, or other family members could then become the limited partners and hold the remainder of the partnership's assets in this form.

Pension limited partnership. Retirement plans are also subject to seizure by creditors and the government. A pension limited partnership (PLP) can make assets difficult or impossible to attack. Your IRA custodian, pension plan, or Keogh becomes a limited partner in a limited partnership that has a totally independent person (someone other than a relative or employee) or corporation acting as sole general partner.

The PLP's general partner is free to invest your pension assets anywhere in the world. Again, I highly recommend seeking the advice of a professional before establishing this type of asset protection structure.

Charitable trusts. This type of arrangement is usually for people with very large estates. For example, one of the companies I work with specializes in setting up the following scenario: You put a million dollars or so into a charitable trust. This becomes a tax-deductible donation to your favorite charity. The trust then transfers the money to a Nevada corporation, which is, in turn, wired to an offshore trust. The offshore trust transfers the funds to another corporation, which is owned by a foreign national who "loans" the money back to the original "donor" at a competitive rate. The loan is not considered income, and thus, is not taxable. Sound complicated? Don't try this at home. That's why the professionals who specialize in these arrangements make the big bucks. Check out the *Directory of Consumer Credit Services* by contacting: Financial Dynamics, P.O. Box 51581, Riverside, CA 92517-2581.

Business trusts. The business trust, also known as the "Massachusetts trust," "common-law trust," "contractual company," unincorporated business organization (UBO)," "constitutional trust," "business trust organization," and many other names, is one of the hottest asset protection techniques to come down the pike in recent years. Be careful with this one, however, because there are a lot of promoters out there hyping the benefits of these structures with overstated claims and overpriced fees. They can be useful strategies, however, if structured properly. Once again, seek the assistance of a professional.

CHAPTER FOUR

Banking Alternatives

Prior to 1913, a customer deposited real wealth or substance in the form of gold or silver into a bank and received a receipt or "claim check" in return. This receipt could be presented to the bank at any time and the gold or silver (the real wealth or substance) would be returned. This redeemable receipt was an actual claim upon the assets of the bank. Since the redeemable receipts were good as gold, they were commonly exchanged for goods and services in the local community of the bank, because the eventual holder could always claim the precious metal at the bank.

This old-style banking worked exceptionally well for the depositors for over 120 years, and it placed some restrictions on itself, which was very good for the local community he country as well.

dent John Adams remarked that "the only honest bank is a bank of deposit." Old-style warehouse banks (banks of deposit) operated much differently from modern debt money banking. Modern banking appears to be almost free of charge because your deposits are loaned out about 16 times over at interest. You are not charged a great deal immediately, but you pay just the same in the deflated value of your debt money notes. Since warehouse banks did not loan out their depositors' money for interest, they typically charged 2 percent on deposit and 2 percent on withdrawals and in this way earned an honest living by the service they performed.

Honest warehouse banking vanished in 1913 with the passage of the Federal Reserve Act, an unconstitutional act that took control of our nation's money away from our government and put it in the hands of international financiers.

The Federal Reserve System banks will not maintain your privacy. When you bank with the Federal Reserve System, your records are copied by your bank, and these copies of your records are turned over to the IRS whenever asked for. Also, your bank will seize your account for the IRS under *due process of law*.

The future holds an even greater trap for those still using the Federal Reserve System. The banks and our government plan a major currency exchange and devaluation soon (probably at a ratio of 10 to 1), and plans are already well under way to establish what many believe is going to be a completely cashless society. With no cash, you are at the mercy of Big Brother and the bureaucrats. Your wealth will exist in the computer of the very people who wish to make you an economic slave. If you are not a "good slave," your entire purchasing power can be wiped out at their will. You will not be able to buy or sell without your National ID Transaction Card, a debit card with your Social Security number (SSN) in the bar code.

Anyone not prepared and using bartering and warehouse banking will suffer the effects of the currency devaluation and be forced to use a debit card in order to survive.

Fortunately, there are alternatives to Federal Reserve System banks. For information about establishing a secret numbered account in the United States, with as much privacy as Swiss, Cayman Island, or other offshore havens, contact: National Coin Exchange (NCE), 33838 S.E. Kelso Rd., Suite 2, P.O. Box 596, Boring, OR 97009. This company offers a warehouse banking system as described above. Here are some advantages of using the NCE warehouse banking system:

- Deposits can be held in gold or silver, which are historically the most stable stores of value.
- The records of your account are absolutely private. No third-party records are kept. The NCE does NOT divulge the existence of your account to ANYONE.
- Each account is numbered for your protection.
- You are free to realize a federal reserve note (dollar) gain if the market value of your precious metal rises above the price for which you purchased it.
- The NCE can pay your bills for you with NO paper (or electronic) trail, which is traceable back to you.
- You are outside Big Brother's coming cashless society.
- The account is not subject to seizure by the IRS or any other governmental agency, due to our right to associate to redress government under the First Amendment.

FOREIGN HAVENS

The government would like you to believe that the only people who put money into foreign bank accounts are tax evaders, drug dealers, and organized crime figures. They would like for Americans to think that there is something inherently sinister about wanting to invest or save their money in another country. Nothing could be further from the truth.

As important as financial privacy may be, there are several other important reasons to open a foreign bank account. Here are five reasons for opening an offshore account:

1. the declining value of the U.S. dollar
2. foreign investment opportunities
3. asset protection
4. banking safety
5. tax advantage

Given the unstable nature of the U.S. economy, all of the above are perfectly valid reasons for wanting to place a portion of your assets in foreign accounts.

Contrary to popular belief, it is not necessary to travel overseas to open an account in a foreign bank. A foreign bank in your city may be able to set up a "correspondent account" at a branch outside the United States. You can also open a foreign bank account by mail. Banks in every part of the world, including Switzerland, Canada, and many other countries, conduct business by mail every day. It's easier to open a bank account by mail in many countries than it is in the United States.

If you are willing to do some traveling, you can visit Canada, the Bahamas, the Cayman Islands, or Bermuda and set up your foreign bank account in person.

Switzerland is considered to be the bastion of banking privacy. The country's bank secrecy laws make it the most valued haven of international investing. Switzerland is also a neutral, politically and economically stable country, which is why Swiss bank accounts are preferred over accounts in other countries.

Other countries that are known for their bank secrecy laws include:

1. Bermuda
2. the Cayman Islands
3. the Bahamas
4. Canada
5. Mexico
6. Austria

The *Directory of Consumer Credit Services* contains a comprehensive listing of foreign banks as well as the names of several attorneys and companies that can help you establish an off-shore account. Contact: Financial Dynamics, 4020 Chicago Ave., Suite 107, Riverside, CA 92507.

CHAPTER FIVE

Alternate Identities

I'd like to caution you before using these techniques to do so prudently. As I mentioned in the disclaimer, some of these methods are subject to misuse if used with the wrong motivation. One unscrupulous individual was found to be using this technique to run up bills of tens of thousands of dollars under several different credit identities simultaneously, then charging them all off through bankruptcy. Then he would start over again using several accomplices to open different accounts. It is my sincere hope that you use this information wisely and that you consult a professional before making any major decisions concerning your life and finances.

Creating an alternate identity is a time-honored tradition in the United States and one of our most neglected freedoms. Ever since the early Native Americans used the ritual of name-changing to denote accomplishment, Americans have changed their names in order to gain some form of success and/or acceptance. Some of the traditional reasons for a change of name include:

- to create a marketable stage name (i.e., Whoopie Goldberg)
- to avoid ridicule or obvious ethnic classification
- to make a political or religious statement (i.e. Malcolm X, Muhammad Ali, etc.)
- for simplification (such as with names that are difficult to spell or pronounce)
- to create a dignified or impressive name or "title"
- to avoid or utilize historical name associations (i.e., Hitler)
- to escape

Here are a few additional ideas and suggestions that may help you along your road to a happy destiny:

- Remember, it is not illegal to change your identity as long as you do not do so for criminal purposes and do not lie on government forms about having had a previous identity.
- Voluntarily becoming a "missing person" is not a criminal offense. Most police departments don't even investigate such reports unless there is a warrant out for arrest or evidence indicating the possibility of kidnapping, suicide, or foul play.
- Choose a new name with different initials. The farther away from your original name, the better
- Practice saying your new name aloud. Become comfortable with your new identity and avoid references to your old life.
- Practice writing your new signature to overcome panic or hesitation.
- Use a post office box or mail drop for most of your correspondence. NOTE: Do not use a post office box or mail drop when applying for credit or bank accounts, however, as they have a computerized listing of such addresses, which will mark your application as "potentially fraudulent."

THE BIRTH CERTIFICATE

The foundation for almost any other kind of ide
for American citizens is the birth certificate. Over ?
and local vital records offices issue birth certificates with no
uniform standards for issuance procedures or quality control.
Birth certificates are easily counterfeited, obtained through
impersonation, or created from stolen legitimate blank forms.

Most Americans are issued two legally valid birth documents. The first is the hospital record of birth. When a child is
born at a hospital, the attending physician will fill out a short
piece of paper with the time of birth, sex of the baby, and type
of birth. Later on, after everything is finished in the recovery
room, the doctor will fill out that particular hospital's standard
birth certificate form. This form will have the name of the hospital, the location of the hospital, and some very basic information on it. The parents' names and ages at the time of birth
are shown, along with the child's name, sex, date, and time of
birth. At the bottom are places for the doctor's signature and the
signature of a witness. The hospital's own seal will usually be
on this form.

This hospital birth certificate is then notarized and submitted to the County Recorder's Office. Then, in some cases, the
county recorder will send out a state-issued birth certificate to
the parents. On a monthly or quarterly basis, the county
recorder will forward a listing of all births that occurred during
that period to the central state Vital Statistics Bureau. So, for a
period of many months, the infant may not have his birth
record on file at the central state Vital Statistics Bureau. The
notarized photocopy of the hospital birth record is generally
destroyed by the local registrar once the birth has been entered
into the record book.

In 1976, the Federal Advisory Committee on False
Identification (FACFI) of the Justice Department pointed out
that false identification was a serious national problem. In
1984, the Task Force on Criminal Implications of False
Identification, sponsored by Laws at Work (LAW), a national

tizen's association interested in law enforcement issues, endorsed a broad range of proposed actions, including a national review of birth certificate systems and practices.

The committee made the following findings:

- A birth certificate is the key to opening many doors in our society—from citizenship privileges to Social Security benefits. Such certificates can then be used as "breeder" documents to obtain driver's licenses, passports, Social Security cards, or other documents with which to create a false identity.
- The birth certificate is also a key to creating a false identity and thus has great value for undocumented aliens who seek fraudulent citizenship, ineligible applicants who seek jobs or benefits, credit defrauders, fugitives, terrorists, and drug smugglers. Individuals can obtain a valid birth certificate through theft, purchase, borrowing, or applying and then impersonate the real owner. They may produce, steal, or buy a counterfeit or altered document.
- Issuance of birth certificates is a state function, but almost 7,000 local registrar's offices also issue certificates. The resulting multitude of certificate forms, official seals, and signatures (an estimated 10,000 nationwide) makes it extremely difficult for user agency workers to detect false documents.
- Privacy and security safeguards to protect birth records from unauthorized disclosures vary from state to state. In some cases, this is attributable to a lack of state statutes on privacy of vital record information. Ten states allow the public open access to vital records. Even in the restricted states, however, ID is often not required. Weak physical security of forms and records and the use of non-safety paper for certificates create additional vulnerabilities.
- Local offices that issue most birth certificates are even more vulnerable. They are less likely than their state offices to have safety paper, a standard state form, adequate security, or to marked "deceased" on birth certificates for dead registrants.

- A variety of measures to fight fraud have been developed. Many states limit local issuance, and many now provide a standard state birth certificate form to their local offices and use safety paper, or plan to do so. It is also becoming increasingly common to match birth and death records.

BIRTH CERTIFICATE FRAUD

"They are definitely being used for fraudulent purposes. We may be seeing the tip of the iceberg. Birth certificates are needed for our life-style. A person needs a birth certificate to participate in society. For false identity, it is what is needed."
—A New England fraud investigator

Birth certificate fraud involves one or more of the following illegal acts: stealing, transferring, or selling valid birth certificates; counterfeiting, selling, or using bogus documents; using or selling altered documents; and using someone else's valid certificate by impersonating the owner.

Impersonation is the most common method used to obtain a birth certificate for fraudulent purposes. In some areas, counterfeiting is a big business. Using a counterfeit birth certificate is the second most common method of committing birth certificate fraud. Alteration of a valid certificate is the third most frequent method used. Theft is the least used method of birth certificate fraud.

The following cases illustrate the impersonation method of committing birth certificate fraud:

- Many years ago, a baby died in infancy. Recently, a young man under the age of 20 and employed as a caretaker in a local cemetery requested from a registrar's office a copy of the birth certificate of the dead infant. Since this state considers birth records public information and allows practically anyone to request and obtain anyone else's birth certificate, he was able to get the dead infant's birth certificate. He attempted to open a bank account using the identity of the long-deceased infant. Much to his surprise, he was arrested after being recognized by the bank teller, who was the mother of the dead infant.

- A supplemental security income (SSI) beneficiary, age 41, was using fake medical data under false names to receive multiple SSI payments. The subject obtained death certificates of two persons, both born within one or two years of his birth. With these, he then obtained birth certificates from the counties of their birth. He used these birth certificates to obtain Department of Motor Vehicles (DMV) identification. He then took the birth certificate and DMV identification for one person to the Social Security Administration (SSA) office to apply for a Social Security number. He obtained another SSN from another SSA office using the other set of identification. Once the false identities were established, he filed multiple claims for SSI in different SSA offices.

- Between April 1985 and June 1986, a legally blind escaped convict fraudulently obtained at least three SSN cards and $1,313 in SSI disability payments. He used fraudulently obtained legitimate birth certificates to establish fictitious identities prior to filing for the SSN cards. He then filed for SSI disability using the false ID and newly acquired SSN. An investigation revealed that he was a fugitive from a federal correctional facility in California, where he had been serving a 15-year sentence for fraudulently obtaining more than $140,000 in SSI payments over a 7-year period. He had established at least 38 known fictitious identities.

Many other cases were reported by registrars and other investigators illustrating fraud through counterfeiting and alteration of documents. For example:

- A counterfeiter in a southwest city printed birth certificates on safety paper. He sold the certificates for $40 to $50 each, and they were resold by a trafficker in false ID for $1,000 to $1,500 each.

— A SSA employee invented 25 fictitious beneficiaries over a period of 10 years. To do this, she took a photocopied birth certificate from a legitimate beneficiary file, whited-out the real name, and typed in the fictitious information on the birth certificate. She then made a photocopy of the altered certificate for the fake beneficiary's file. Before being discovered, she received approximately $360,000.

Career criminals include:

— those who use false identities to engage in such activities as drug smuggling, insurance fraud, cashing bad checks, counterfeiting and/or selling birth and other documents, entering sham marriages for a price, credit card or bank fraud, securities fraud, money laundering, organized crime, and illegal departure from and entry into the country
— terrorists, espionage agents, and fugitives who use false documents to avoid identification and detection
— ineligible beneficiaries who habitually use the fraudulent paper route to obtain such government benefits as Aid to Families with Dependent Children (AFDC) based on nonexistent children, other public assistance, unemployment insurance, SSI, Social Security (i.e., retirement, survivor or disability payments), college grants and loans, and sometimes duplicate benefits under different identities
— some employees of issuing or user agencies who, by illegally issuing or accepting birth certificates, facilitate birth certificate fraud by the above kinds of criminals

Some otherwise law-abiding citizens also get caught up in using altered or other illegal birth certificates to gain privileges or avoid legal penalties. Common examples include: parents of minors whose birth record ages are changed to make them eligible for Little League teams; minors to get a driver's license or buy alcoholic beverages; adults who change their recorded age for what is called "vanity fraud" or to speed up or delay retirement, Medicare, or Social Security benefits; people who want to escape a bad credit record, delinquent debts, or personal obligations; and those who assume an alternate identity to avoid taxes, child support, or fines.

Illegal aliens typically use fraudulent birth certificates for gaining a legal status, benefit, or privilege to which they are not entitled. Those who misuse birth certificates seek to:

— become a U.S. citizen or legal alien
— get a Social Security card to work or to collect unemployment benefits
— become eligible for welfare benefits
— obtain a passport
— get a lower college tuition rate or certain college grants and loans

Obtaining an Official Birth Certificate
"Almost anyone can go over to the State and get someone else's birth certificate."
—a welfare fraud investigator in an "open record" state

At least five states—California, Massachusetts, Minnesota, Vermont, and Washington—have laws that classify them as "open record" states. These are states in which, according to a local registrar, "By law, the original birth registration is a public record. Anyone can see it and get a copy of it. We have no authority to question."

These five "open" states allow any individual with the minimum necessary information to apply for and obtain a copy of anyone's birth certificate. Offices in these states generally do not require any ID from the applicant. States with protected record statutes allow copies to be issued only to certain categories of persons. Typically, those eligible include registrants over 18, parents, guardians, or legal representatives. However, even in the stricter states, ID is rarely required at the State Registrar's Office.

The book *Paper Trip II* warns against requesting a birth certificate in certain states and cities and advises its readers, ". . . that you not get discouraged that your efforts appear stymied in a particular area. Go to the next county—or state—and try again. Nine times out of 10 you won't believe how easy it is."

All states, whether protected or not, are vulnerable to birth certificate fraud because ID is seldom required, fraud prevention has a low priority, particularly in local offices, and death records can frequently be obtained.

Applying for a Birth Certificate by Mail or Telephone

Most states use application forms for the 15 to 20 percent of applicants who walk into the state office and request a birth certificate. In the large majority of requests to the state office, which are made by mail or telephone, application forms are generally not used.

The situation is reversed in local offices: walk-ins constitute about 60 percent of all applicants, and applications are generally required. The remaining 40 percent who request a copy by mail or phone do not fill out applications.

Applicants who mail or telephone in their requests, without application forms, usually do not have to give any identification or even provide their signature. Mail requests are generally the easiest mode of request because there is no opportunity for the requester to be questioned as with walk-ins and even phone-ins.

In the last several years, a growing number of state and local registrars have begun to accept applications by telephone. This procedure has been facilitated by computer technology. Registrar clerks key the information given by the telephone applicants into a terminal, including a credit card number to cover the fee. Since there is no way of verifying that the caller is the same person whose name is on the credit card or, for that matter, is eligible for the requested certificate, impersonation by telephone is as easy as by mail.

Even if your request is made in person, the applications are all relatively easy to complete. Among the questions contained in nearly all the forms, only one is not easily known to an outsider: the mother's maiden name. But this can be obtained from a death certificate (which will be discussed in the next section).

Most birth certificate applications fail to ask for such items as the hospital or address at which the registrant was born, the full name at birth, or the applicant's signature. Even when the forms do contain the above items, the applicant is usually not required to answer every question. In some offices, the applicant's signature is optional.

The Paper Trip

One of the more publicized methods of obtaining a new birth certificate is known as the "paper trip" method, named after the popular books on alternate identity available from Paladin Press and other publishers.

This method is also known as the "infant identity" method, as it involves using a birth certificate of someone who died at a very young age. Although I personally find this particular technique to be rather morbid, I will describe it briefly, for informational purposes only.

The infant identity method requires that you find the identity of a child who was born near your own birth date, but who died a few years later before accumulating a paper trail with the Social Security Administration, Department of Motor Vehicles, FBI, welfare departments, etc. Some people locate such an identity by visiting a graveyard or by going through old newspapers. It is important not to use someone who died in a highly publicized plane or train crash. This is because many other privacy seekers will have also requested these same birth certificates many times before. If one particular birth certificate is requested too often, the state Vital Statistics Bureau will flag it for non-release or trigger an investigation into why it is being requested so often.

Another pitfall of this method is what is called cross-referencing of birth and death records. Usually this will occur at the county level, but it is also done at the state level in many places. When a person dies in the same county of their birth, the county registrar will stamp "deceased" on the person's birth certificate. In statewide cross-referencing, a similar process will occur at the state Vital Statistics Bureau for all people who were born and died in that state. There are two possible ways around these problems:

1. Look through old newspapers for a child who died in an isolated incident. Pick a child who would be about your age today. First, write for the death certificate. The death certificate will let you know if the child was born in the same county or state of death. You can then request the birth certificate. If the state only cross-references on a countywide basis, the identity is okay to use if the death occurred in another county. If the state cross-references on a statewide basis, you should find another name.

   In most states, both the central Vital Statistics Bureau and local county office issue birth certificates. If statewide cross-referencing of birth and death records exist, often it is only done at the central state office and will appear on birth certificates issued from that office. A way around this problem is to write to both the county and state offices for the certificate. You will then have a definitive answer. Another loophole is that states that cross-reference only began doing this with records starting at a certain date. There have been too many people born and already dead to go back very far. The best protection is to find a child who was born in one state and died in another. Many large cities operate independent Vital Statistics Bureaus for all births and deaths within city limits. Statewide or county-wide cross-referencing will probably not affect them.

2. In most cases, a new identity can be built around a "created" birth record, properly backed up by supportive identification. The ultimate privacy seeker can then obtain all of the state-issued identification needed—driver's license, credit cards, state ID card, voter registration card, etc. After a year or so, a passport can even be obtained. So, the first question for the privacy seeker when cross-referencing becomes commonplace is, "Must my birth record be verifiable?" In most cases, the answer is no.

Blank Birth Certificates

It is perfectly legal to obtain blank birth certificates from one of several mail order suppliers. The best documents are printed on parchment paper, which gives it an official appearance. By using an embosser and rubber seal, you can create a document that is indistinguishable from an officially issued hospital birth certificate.

As a result of the False Identification Crime Control Act of 1982, privately issued identification documents now require the phrase "Not a Government Document" on the face of the document if it bears the birth date or age of the person named. Presumably, if the document does not show an age or birth date, the phrase is not required. Many issuers of ID by mail have found ways to help the ultimate privacy seeker get around this annoying little formality. In some cases, the disclaimer is printed on an expanded portion of the document, which can be cut off with a pair of scissors without interfering with the face of the document itself.

Some people have used White-Out correction fluid to cover the "Not a Government Document" disclaimer. Then a photocopy of the birth certificate is made onto yellow parchment paper, which can be purchased from any stationary or office supply store. The new document (without the disclaimer) is ready to be trimmed down to certificate size. A typewriter is used to fill in the blanks, or the information can be handwritten with a fountain pen. If you are also using a baptismal or confirmation certificate for backup identification, do not use the same typewriter font to complete this document. Also, be sure to use a different type of paper for additional supporting documents. Another tip: if you are past a certain age, do not use a modern electric typewriter to fill in the blanks on your vertificate. Dig up an old manual model instead.

The completed document is then stamped with an embossing seal from the hospital of birth and rubber stamped with the words "Original Document" or "Certified Copy" in red ink.

The easiest way to get a Social Security number is through the mail. This can be accomplished if the birth date on the birth certificate makes the applicant appear to be under the age of 18. This eliminates the requirement to apply in person at the Social Security Administration office for a face-to-face interview (interrogation). The SSA needs one other piece of ID, such as a church confirmation certificate, school ID, or transcript, insurance policy, health insurance card, report card, medical records, or government ID card.

Applying for a Social Security card in person requires an explanation of why you are getting the card at such a late age. There are only three explanations that make sense:

1. You have been in a prison or mental hospital since childhood.
2. You have been out of the country since childhood.
3. You have been a prostitute, drug dealer, vagrant, or criminal since childhood.

In completing the birth certificate, the "residence at time child was born" should be a city or town close to where the hospital is located.

The physician's signature is usually scribbled and impossible to read, except for the initials "M.D." after the signature. The hospital administrator's signature is usually easier to read and signed with a different color pen.

The hospital embossing seal is applied to the certificate to make it "feel" authentic. A lot of pressure must be applied when squeezing the embossing seal to make a readable impression. A rubber stamp is also necessary to validate the document. The rubber stamp should be applied on a slight angle, not perfectly straight. A red stamp pad can be bought at any office supply or drug store. The SSA and Department of Motor Vehicles won't accept a birth certificate without an embossed seal and rubber stamp.

The final step is to "age" the certificate by placing it in an oven or toaster oven for about three minutes. By setting the broiler to 500 degrees and placing the certificate on aluminum foil about two inches under the heating element, the document will take on a brittle, yellow appearance. Another technique is to fold up the certificate, place it in the bottom of your shoe, and walk around on it for about a week. (The examiners at the SSA and DMV get suspicious when they see a new-looking document that's supposed to be 17 years old.)

CHAPTER SIX

Vital Records Cross-Referencing

There would be a time delay loophole in the birth/death matching. Updating would occur probably only once per month, which would allow a clever [paper] tripper time enough to obtain a birth certificate of a recently deceased person.

—Paper Trip I

For those who must have a verifiable birth record, it is important to understand how a potential vital records cross-referencing system would (or would not) work in the United States. Remember, there are more than 7,000 offices authorized to handle and manufacture birth and death records. In some areas, they are considered public documents open to all; in others, these records are closed and available only to state workers and other authorized personnel.

The basic idea of nationwide cross-referencing works like this. When a person dies in one state who was born in another state, the state where the person died would send a copy of the death certificate to the state where the person was born. This death certificate would then be physically attached to the birth record. Anyone who later requested this birth certificate would be refused, or made to show cause as to why it should be released.

Here's the problem with this theory. When a doctor issues a death certificate, one of his primary concerns is making an accurate identification of the victim. This is done initially by comparing any pieces of identification on the victim with the body. If someone who knows the victim can be found in a timely fashion, this person serves to buttress the initial identification. If no additional information as to the birthplace of the victim can be found quickly, the death certificate will be filled out with the information available.

Certain privacy seekers have stumbled upon this fact when researching death records for a suitable candidate. Often the death certificate will not contain the birthplace of the deceased, particularly if the deceased died in an accident. This same fact will cause a lot of holes in any future cross-referencing system. But these are not the only holes that will be created.

Before a state will agree to affix another state's death certificate to one of its birth records, a lot of legal conditions must be met. This is because the act of mating these two records effectively declares this person "dead." The state could face massive amounts of legal damage if it accepts another state's death record and accidentally "kills" someone who is quite alive and well. And rest assured this would happen with some regularity if a nationwide cross-referencing system came into being. There are just too many people with similar names and birth dates to avoid a lot of mix-ups. Secondly, some states will not accept other states' certificates of death as legal records because they will not contain enough information. Clearly, the states would have to agree to use a standard-issue death certificate form and use the same death certificate issuance procedures.

Another problem with this system is that for it to be effective, both the central state Vital Records Bureau and the local county registrar must be sent a copy of the death record. This also entails a lot of expense, because for every death certificate received, a vital records search would have to be performed at both the state vital records office and the county registrar level to make sure the deceased was actually "born." In addition, to cope with the liability problem mentioned earlier, the state receiving the death certificate will probably also want independent confirmation of the death by a relative or friend of the deceased.

As one can imagine, a large time delay would be involved in any such nationwide scheme. Even if it was done, the time delay would be on the order of many weeks and would allow any privacy seeker a large "window of opportunity" to procure these records. The prospect of a nationwide data base to handle this function is similarly remote. One need only look to the British to get an idea of the fiasco that would result.

The British developed a centralized national voter list back in the 1970s. In theory, the central computer is supposed to know who is authorized to vote. The names of 45 million people are stored on this data base, and hundreds of thousands of names are added each year. Inputs into the system can be made at hundreds of offices nationwide. The end result is that the system is notorious for creating people who don't exist and removing people from the voting rolls who are entitled to vote. This happens because so many people have similar names and birth dates. An active data base that is so large and constantly changing is subject to abundant inaccuracies. But it is one thing to tell a person he cannot vote and quite another to tell him that he has been declared dead.

The ultimate privacy seeker has a number of choices when it comes to selecting a new birth record. If you have created an entirely new identity, it is best to create records that cannot be traced. Here is where hospital and church birth documents have a definite advantage. If you use a hospital birth record from a hospital that has long since closed, the ability of anyone to disprove your record's veracity is next to impossible. The same can be said of deceased midwives or doctors. The same is also true if you become a pastor in another name and issue your own baptismal certificates. Over the years many churches and parishes have closed down or burned down and the records have been lost. If you claim to have a baptismal certificate from one of these services, no one can say otherwise. A state-issued birth certificate can always be traced to the originator of the record.

All state-issued birth certificates that come from a state's central Vital Statistics Bureau will contain a state birth number. These numbers are important to be aware of because the federal government, in an attempt to reduce passport and Social Security number fraud, has trained its people to recognize these numbers.

First, a state birth number will not appear on a certificate issued by a local county registrar. If a person applies for a passport, one of the first checks the passport clerk makes is to look at where the state birth certificate was issued. If it came from the state Vital Statistics Bureau, it should have a birth number on it, and this number is written down on the application form. If it was issued by a county registrar, the certificate will only carry a local registrar's file number on it. Any mismatch will immediately alert the passport clerk to possible identity fraud and cause her to retain the certificate.

According to the book *Reborn in the USA* by Trent Sands, the United States uses a common system of birth certificate numbers due to an agreement reached among the states years ago. For example:

1/34-55-023343

The first digit is always a "1"—this shows that you were born in the United States. The next two digits represent the state of birth:"34" is Ohio. The next two digits represent the year of birth: "55" means that you were born in 1955. The last six digits represent the state file number, which is a random sequential number.

ADDITIONAL DOCUMENTATION

One of the first rules of law enforcement officers states, "When any doubt exists, ask for supportive identification and look particularly for any document a year or two old. Most completely forged identification has little supportive identification and most of it is very new."

The Baptismal Certificate

Most state and federal government agencies will accept a valid baptismal certificate as proof of birth. In order for it to be accepted as valid, the baptismal certificate must have been issued within a few months of the child's birth and it must show the parents' names, the child's birth date and birthplace, the date of baptism, and the name and location of the church. It also must bear the signature and either seal or stamp of the church official issuing the document. More importantly, since it was supposed to have been issued a few months after you were born, it must look as old as you are. A brand new baptismal certificate straight out of a mail order catalog will definitely arouse suspicion at your local DMV or Social Security Administration. The baptismal certificate can be "aged" using the previously described methods.

Baptismal certificates can be obtained either by mail or through a religious supply store. Some individuals have even started their own churches through one of the many mail order ministries that advertise in the back of national tabloid newspapers. Many of these papers also advertise ID kits, blank certificates, diplomas, and mail order degrees.

The baptismal certificate can be used along with another piece of identification to obtain a Social Security card or driver's license. The other form of ID can be a birth certificate, church confirmation certificate, school records, insurance card, or utility bill. If the birth date on the baptismal certificate shows you to be age 17 or under, the Social Security Administration will issue an official card through the mail. This eliminates the requirement to apply in person at their office for questioning.

Confirmation Certificate

A church confirmation certificate can be used as an additional form of documentation, along with a birth certificate or baptismal certificate. The confirmation ceremony usually takes place at age 12, so the date on the certificate should be 12 years from the date of birth. Once again, an embossed church seal, along with the proper "aging," will add the required authenticity to the document.

Driver's License

Using a birth certificate, baptismal (or confirmation) certificate, and a Social Security card, getting a driver's license and other supportive identification is easy. The easiest place to get a new driver's license is in a small town. Clerks in small town DMV offices are seldom trained to detect false identification documents. Besides, with more than 7,000 different types of birth documents issued from various hospitals, state offices, and county recorders, it is virtually impossible for a DMV clerk from any office to know how every document is supposed to look.

One of the common obstacles the ultimate privacy seeker may face when trying to obtain a new driver's license is how to respond when a clerk asks, "Why didn't you get your license when you were a teenager?" Many people respond by indicating that they are from a big city (like New York or San Francisco) and always used public transportation. Others simply state that they have never learned to drive before or have been living out of the country. Some individuals have obtained fake driver's licenses from another state or country and have traded the old license in for a new one. Canada, for example, does not trade computer information with the United States, and an authentic looking Canadian driver's license cannot be verified by motor vehicle agencies in the United States.

Many state licensing agencies require one or two thumbprints on their driver's license applications. Many privacy seekers have expressed their concern over this practice and have hesitated to apply for an official driver's license for fear of some type of fingerprint cross-referencing. Here are some interesting facts to consider regarding driver's license fingerprinting:

— The fingerprint does not appear on the driver's license itself. Department of Motor Vehicles fingerprints (usually a single thumbprint) are not classified in any way, nor are they sent to the FBI for classification. The FBI does not have time to classify or run a check on the prints of every motor vehicle license or state identification applicant. The main reason for this practice is as a psychological deterrent to intimidate potential alternate identity seekers.

— Smart privacy seekers often make a practice of giving a totally worthless print. This is accomplished by creating an indistinguishable smudge or smear with no useful characteristics for identification. They accomplish this by pressing harder than necessary and twisting the finger while the print is being made. Having the fingertip surface somewhat oily also helps. Most clerks have had no fingerprint training and will not even realize that you're really "giving them the finger."

— Certain more cunning individuals have gone so far as to spray the finger or thumb area beforehand with New Skin (a spray-on first-aid "bandage" available at your local drugstore). The individual then presses another finger against the finger (or thumb) to be printed, thus creating a false impression.

— I have heard that some people have even taken a razor blade and actually etched permanent scars or shaved the skin off of the printed area to distort the identifying characteristics.

A driver's license is generally accepted as a legitimate piece of identification. It looks extremely bare unless supported by the usual mishmash of other cards carried in a person's wallet.

the usual mishmash of other cards carried in a person's wallet. You will note that many driver's licenses have an indication on them whether they are new or renewed. If it is a new license and can not be supported by extensive foundation documentation, it tends to cause suspicion in the law enforcement community and can make it extremely difficult for you to get credit or loans, as banks have learned that it is best to wait until you have been around long enough to at least renew your driver's license before taking your word on any major transaction.

The way around this is to back up your primary ID with believable secondary paper.

Business Cards

For about $20, you can get 500 very impressive business cards printed up at a quick printer, stating that you are anything from president of a major corporation to Secretary of State. You don't need any ID or qualifying documents to have business cards printed, yet many people consider a business card as official identification. After all, who would bother to print up phony business cards?

Library Card

Library cards are very easy to obtain, normally requiring two pieces of identification, one of which can be an envelope addressed to the proposed reader at his "home address."

School IDs

It is possible to get a legitimate school ID from most universities and junior colleges in the United States by taking one or more classes (or just by signing up for a class) at the school's extension program. Most schools do not require you to be a full-time student in order to get the ID card because it is required for library privileges and student activities. You can usually pick up other support documents in the school bookstore or on campus to help give the impression that you are a serious student. The school ID can also entitle you to many student discounts and other benefits.

Although no law requires you to carry a Social Security card, an authentic-looking card will definitely add credibility to any wallet. Engraved metal Social Security cards can be obtained from street vendors and mail order companies for a few dollars. Other companies offer realistic looking "Social Insecurity Cards" for novelty purposes, which can be torn, burned, or otherwise modified to eliminate irregularities or disclaimers (such as "Not a Government Document").

Photographs
Always carry pictures of your wife, your kids, your dog, someone else's wife, someone else's kids, etc.

Membership Cards
Join groups such as the Sheriff's Athletic Association, Citizen's Rights Council, or Rotary Club etc. You can also purchase these membership cards from mail order companies or make your own using desktop publishing or a local print shop.

Credit Cards
Once an ID has been established and you have followed some basic rules, it is possible to get a secured credit card with little or no credit history. A Visa or MasterCard from a major bank can give you instant credibility (they don't have to know it's a secured card with a $100 credit limit).

OPENING A BANK ACCOUNT

Now that you have a driver's license or state ID card, it is possible to open a checking or savings account. Most banks require at least two pieces of identification and prefer one to be a driver's license and the other to be a credit card. Some banks will allow you to open an account with a driver's license (or state ID card) and a Social Security number.

If you've ever had a checking account closed "with cause," you're likely to be listed in the data base of one of several organizations that compile this type of information for subscribing

nizations that compile this type of information for subscribing banks and other financial institutions. Before you open a new account, your bank will check with such an organization to determine if there have been problems with your accounts in the past. ChexSystems and Telecredit are the most widely used of these services. ChexSystems is a deposit account verification service for financial institutions. The company is a subsidiary of Deluxe, the company known for printing checks for most checking accounts. Although this information does not show up on credit reports, it is reported to banks when a person tries to open up a new account. Its purpose is to inform inquiring institutions whether a prospective account holder has a record of prior closed accounts for nonsufficient funds (NSF) activity. These records are normally retrieved by the subject's name and SSN.

This information is verified when the subscribing bank contacts ChexSystems by telephone and provides the operator with the following identifying information:

1. last name
2. first name
3. middle initial
4. joint or individual account—when the inquiry is for a joint account, identifying information must be provided for the joint applicant (Do not apply for a joint checking account. You may add the joint applicant to the account later as an additional signer with little problem.)
5. whether the applicant has lived in the same state for five years (The actual address is not provided to ChexSystems unless you have been at your current address for less than five years.)
6. Social Security number

The ChexSystems operator will enter the above information into her computer system. The response may range from "that number was issued out of California on or about February of 1991, and we have no record" to "that number was issued out of California on or about February of 1991, and we have record of NSF activity." The state of issuance and date of issuance peri-

group listings from the SSA. ChexSystems also receives a SSA Death Master File Listing, which is a listing of Social Security numbers whose account holders are deceased.

In your case, the new accounts officer will hear Chex-Systems reply, "No Record." This simply means that they have no record of any closed accounts matching your name and Social Security number.

Telecredit is another account verification service used mainly in the retail world (by merchants). Equifax owns Telecredit ,and checks that are not satisfied and are on their data base will be reported on an Equifax credit report. In order to get your name removed you must negotiate with the originating financial institution.

A consumer file with one of these companies is a negative file—only those who have had financial privileges terminated "with cause" are included in these files. "Cause" includes overdraft abuse, ATM abuse (such as empty envelope deposits), check kiting, etc. Your name can stay in their files for 5 years. All account verification companies are subject to the rules of the Fair Credit Reporting Act. You can submit a written dispute or just a request for a report, which will be provided free of charge. When requesting a report, include your name, SSN, driver's license number, and addresses used during the past five years to:

ChexSystems
3050 S. 35th Street, Suite A
Phoenix, AZ 85034

Telecredit Consumer Affairs
5301 Idlewild
Tampa, FL 33634

PASSPORTS

Mr. Molinaro, a 46-year-old Santa Ana, California, resident obtained a birth certificate from a long deceased northern California man and then used it to obtain a California driver's

California man and then used it to obtain a California driver's license in the deceased man's name. He then applied for a U.S. passport days later using the license information as the primary identification. When he went to San Francisco three weeks later to pick up his passport from the downtown passport office, he was arrested by the FBI and charged with making false statements on a passport application. Instead of looking forward to a new life, Molinaro faced a maximum sentence of five years in prison and a $250,000 fine.

Molinaro's mistake was a basic one. He assumed that the clerk who processed this application would be as "diligent" as the clerk at the motor vehicles department. The passport clerk thought it was rather strange that the applicant was 32 years of age and had a driver's license that was issued only a month ago. The clerk did some checking and found out that the real applicant died more than 30 years ago. The clerk then alerted the U.S. Attorney's Office.

Because the U.S. passport is one of the most valuable documents in the world and is considered proof positive when verifying the identity of the holder, one could expect some verification procedures to be in force. A U.S. passport can be applied for at any of the passport offices in major cities throughout the country, at federal courthouses, or at certain post offices.

All passport applications must be submitted in person before an authorized official. The reason for this is that immediate certification is done on a subjective basis.

In order to be eligible for a U.S. passport, it is necessary to prove your identity and citizenship. This is usually done by showing a birth certificate or other proof of citizenship and an ID that is recognized by the official and contains a picture that fits the physical description and signature of the owner, such as a driver's license, to verify identity.

Passports are not usually cross-referenced with birth or death records except in cases where the agent in charge suspects fraud is involved. The agent has the authority to call the state office where the birth certificate was issued or call witnesses or relatives listed on the application form. If these calls are initiat-

ply be made while the applicant is waiting or has been sent home to return later to pick up the passport.

Passports are processed according to the departure date of the applicant. During the summer, the workload increases due to an increase in overseas travel. It is possible to convince the passport office to issue a passport in as little as a day or two if evidence can be shown that there is a strict need for such acceleration of procedures, such as an emergency trip due to a death or illness in the family, or an unexpected business matter.

Passport Forgery

The following is a list of methods employed in passport fakery:

— Get a real blank passport and fill it in with whatever you wish.
— Get a real valid passport and print copies using desktop publishing technology.
— Using the paper trip, obtain a new birth certificate and apply for a real passport.
— Remove the photo and signature on a real passport and replace them with your own.
— Take out entire pages and substitute them from one passport to another. This is a bit easier than it used to be, as many countries no longer perforate every page with the passport number.

Passport Safeguards

The majority of passports have a watermark on each page. Therefore, attempts to switch pages may lead to having a different watermark on the switched pages or none at all. Only the true professional forger can create a watermark that can withstand a thorough examination.

The use of ultraviolet light is not a commonplace occurrence at customs checkpoints abroad. This light will show any disturbed sections of the passport pages, including methods by forgers to print on a watermark.

A new form of passport is beginning to be used by various

A new form of passport is beginning to be used by various governments and may be the passport of the future. The new passport is similar to a lot of state driver's licenses in size and appearance. It is coated with a heavy plastic and has a photo and the same information as the present passports. What makes this passport so unique is that it is machine readable. A series of numbers and codes are placed on the bottom section of the card. The card would be checked visually by the customs inspector, then scanned by the computer to ensure that it is valid.

The United States is also supposedly about to begin inserting little magnetic tapes in passports. This tape will then be programmed to be read with a computer reader, and it will contain such information as where and when a person has traveled along with phrases such as "arrest me" or other flag phrases on suspected traffickers. This had been previously accomplished by drawing with ultraviolet (UV) ink on the passport. You may have noticed that passport customs officials will often pass your passport under a black light when you reenter the United States. They are looking for one of these UV flags.

CHAPTER SEVEN

Creating an Alternate Credit File

An alternate credit file is created when the identifying information provided to the credit bureau does not match with an existing credit file. So far, no bureau has come up with a perfect file identification system. That is why you will often see items on your report that belong to someone else with a similar name. In an effort to maintain maximum efficiency, the credit bureaus would rather set up more than one file on a single person than risk merging several people's files into one. This is the "Achilles' heel" that has allowed countless individuals to circumvent the system.

By understanding the identification system used by each of the major bureaus, it is possible to circumvent the identification systems of all of these bureaus simultaneously. This process begins with a file that says, "No Record Found." From this point there are several ways to reestablish credit with a new history of positive information. These techniques have been used by individuals from all walks of life and are so effective in "erasing" bad credit records that some consumer advocates are charging fees of up to $3,000 to set up new credit files for their clients.

An alternate credit file is created by changing the following identifying information:

1. name, address, and Social Security number, or
2. address and Social Security number, or
3. name and address

Due to skip tracing and fraud prevention programs used by the various credit bureaus, methods #1 and #2 are preferable to method #3. With nothing more than a SSN, the credit bureaus can provide the inquirer with a list of names and addresses for anyone in their system who has used the input SSN for any reported credit transaction. These SSN search programs are respectively known as:

AccuSearch (used by Experian)
TRACE (used by TransUnion)
DTEC (used by Equifax)

It is important to create a new credit file in all three major credit bureaus. By changing as many elements of identifying information as possible, you increase your chances of circumventing all three bureaus' identification systems simultaneously.

There are two basic credit report formats. These formats are commonly referred to as consumer disclosure reports and subscriber reports. Consumer disclosure reports are available directly to the consumer from the credit bureau and may be obtained in person or by mail. When creating a new credit file, it is preferable to make your request by mail, since obtaining your report in person requires the presentation of proper identification.

Consumer disclosures obtained by mail do not require the presentation of identification. Experian will provide consumers with a free copy of their credit report once each year. The other bureaus will provide you with a free copy of your report if you have been denied credit within the past 60 days based on information supplied by that particular bureau. Otherwise, the bureaus normally charge a fee of $8 for your report.

Simply write to each of the bureaus and request a copy of your credit report, making sure to enclose the required fee, your complete (new) name, address, Social Security number, date of birth, and copy of utility bill, bank statement, or other documentation linking your name to the address where the credit report is to be sent.

Subscriber reports are generally unavailable to consumers due to credit bureau policy. These reports are obtained from the credit bureaus by such companies as banks, collection agencies, real estate companies, auto dealers, and finance companies. If you have a friend who works in one of these types of companies, you may be able to obtain copies of your reports through him or her. These reports may be retrieved in as few as 35 seconds from the point of input and may range in cost from $8 to $20 each.

If the information supplied to the bureau does not match an existing file, this request for your credit report will create a new credit file. This initial report will read "No Record Found" or "File Search Completed." Subsequent reports will show an inquiry listing the name of the company that requested the original report.

Now that you have a hard copy of your credit report from each of the three major bureaus with a newly created file, it is important to substantiate your new identity. This is done by obtaining a new driver's license or state identification card from your local DMV. In most states, you can simply request a new or duplicate card by stating that your original card was lost, destroyed, or stolen. When completing the new application for a duplicate license, just check the blank that says "Name Change" and fill in the application with your new name. This is done all the time in cases of marriage or divorce, where a woman changes her maiden name to her married name, or vice versa.

THE PAPERLESS PAPER TRIP

Many people have taken advantage of offers by car dealers and mortgage companies for free credit checks over the phone. By simply calling up one of these companies and giving them your new name, address, and Social Security number, they will often run a credit report while you wait. If they tell you that your credit report indicates "No Record Found," "No Record," or "File Search Complete," or if they simply state that you have an "insufficient" credit history, you can rest assured that you have just created a new alternate credit file—with no connection to your previous history. The next time a credit report is run on your new identity, there will be an "inquiry" on the report from the subscriber who ordered the first credit report. From this point, it is simply a matter of adding new credit information to your newly created file, then supplementing it with the necessary documentation as needed.

ADDING NEW CREDIT TO YOUR FILE

The fastest way of adding new credit to a newly created file is to have a friend or relative add you to one of their major credit card accounts as a secondary card holder. This little-known method was discovered by a consultant to undercover agents when they needed to add credibility to their alternate identities. By becoming a secondary or additional card holder on the account of someone with a good credit history, the entire history of that card will be added to your credit file. This method is covered in detail in *Credit Secrets: How to Erase Bad Credit* (available from Paladin Press).

Another way to add credit to your new file is to obtain a secured credit card from one or more major banks that offer a Visa or MasterCard based on your corresponding certificate of deposit. These cards will show up on your credit report just like any other bank credit card, with no indication that they are secured by a deposit.

Next, you can open up a small account at a local jewelry or furniture store. Many of these stores offer instant credit to anyone with a major credit card. Department stores, oil companies, tire shops, and electronic retailers will also give you an account with minimal credit references. By paying all of your new accounts on time, or even early, you can quickly build an excellent credit history and become eligible for overdraft checking accounts, signature lines of credit, auto loans, leases, and mortgage loans.

Actually, it is often easier to purchase a house or car on credit than it is to obtain a credit card. This is because a secured loan, such as an auto or home loan, is backed by collateral. The collateral, or secured property, is usually worth at least 20 to 30 percent more than the amount of the loan and the lender is still the legal owner of the property until the loan has been paid in full. That is also why it is easier to obtain a loan if you offer to make a large down payment. In real estate this is sometimes referred to as the 30/70 rule. You can almost always obtain a real estate loan for 70 percent of the value of the property if you put 30 percent as a down payment. The lender realizes that you are highly unlikely to default on a loan for which you have invested 30 percent of your own money (which you would forfeit if you did not pay off the loan as agreed).

Another way to obtain quick credit, regardless of your credit history, is to find someone with good credit who will cosign the loan for you. By cosigning a loan, the person agrees to take responsibility for the loan if you do not make all of your payments as agreed. This is a major responsibility for anyone to undertake and should not be looked upon lightly. For example, if a person cosigns for someone on an auto loan and the car gets repossessed, the cosigner could be liable for paying the balance on the loan and legal fees resulting from the collection process. Additionally, the loan will show up on the cosigner's credit report, adding to his debt-to-income ratio, and could result in the cosigner being denied credit elsewhere. Any late payments, collection accounts, or other derogatory information regarding the account will be reflected on the cosigner's credit report as well.

A better way of obtaining quick credit, regardless of your previous history, is to obtain a compensating balance loan secured by a savings account or certificate of deposit. Start with at least a thousand dollars, if possible, to get the full benefits of this technique. This is similar to having a secured credit card, except that you simply make a deposit into your local bank or credit union, then after a few days have passed, you borrow money against your savings. This borrowed money can then be placed into a second account in another bank. A few days later, the money is borrowed again and the loan proceeds are placed into a third bank account (at a third bank). A few days later, borrow against this account and place the proceeds into a separate checking account. A week later, write a check for the first payment to each of the three banks where the loans were drawn. A week later, write a second check for another full payment on all three accounts. A week later, make a third full payment on all three loans. Now you will show three bank references with savings accounts, bank loans (paid ahead of time), and a checking account.

CHAPTER EIGHT

Legal Methods of Creating Alternate Identities

The following section provides you with a variety of completely legal techniques for creating alternate identities. By following the letter of the law and obtaining officially sanctioned documents through legitimate channels, you can be free to start over with a new identity, without having to worry about being entangled again in the yoke of bondage.

CHANGING YOUR NAME

I would to God thou and I knew where a commodity of good names were to be bought.

—Shakespeare, *Henry IV*, Pt. I

As an adult citizen of the United States, you have the right to use any name you choose providing that it is not used with the intent to defraud and that it does not interfere with the right of another person (such as using the name of a famous entertainer or public figure).

Every state has at least one method to change an individual's name, but some states have two methods. These are commonly known as court petition and usage. Depending on the state in which you live, both are legal and valid methods. For example, California residents have the right to be known by whatever first and last name they choose.

Court Petition Method

The court petition method is available in all states with fees ranging from $95 to $200 with publishing. A name change by this method is accomplished by completing a form and filing it with the county clerk's office. A short notice is then published in a local newspaper stating that you are changing your name. Unless someone were to object to your name change, it will normally be approved without the necessity of your appearing in court.

Objections to a name change could come from a number of sources and for a variety of reasons, including creditors or ex-spouses who feel you may be trying to skip out on a debt, celebrities who feel your name change may constitute an invasion of their privacy, or even the judge's opinion that you may be requesting the change with the intent to commit fraud.

Usage Method

A name change by the usage method is accomplished by simply using a new name in all aspects of your personal, social, and business life. No court action is necessary, it costs nothing, and it is just as valid as a name changed by court petition. (The purpose of the court petition is simply to give you an "official" record of the change.) California law specifically affirms the right of persons to change their name by the usage method

(Code of Civil Procedure 1279.5a): "Continuation of common law right to change one's name: (a) nothing in this title shall be construed to abrogate the common law right of any person to change one's name."

The practical steps to implement a usage name change are:

1. Contact the various government and business agencies you deal with and change your name on their records. This may include the Department of Motor Vehicles. In California and several other states you may go to the DMV and say, "I have changed my name and would like to have it changed on my driver's license." You must fill out a name change form, take a new photograph and/or thumbprint, and pay the application fee. No other documents are required.

2. Social Security Administration. Go to the local Social Security office and complete a Form SS-5. You will need to show one piece of "acceptable" identification with your new name and a certified copy of the court decree, if applicable, or an additional piece of identification in your new name. Forms of acceptable identification are listed on the SS-5 form for your convenience.

3. Internal Revenue Service. The completed SS-5 form provided to the SSA is automatically forwarded to the IRS. You are not required to contact the IRS yourself. File your next income tax return using your new name.

4. State taxing agencies. Send a letter to the applicable agency explaining your name change and stating your old name and Social Security number. No legal document is required. File your next income tax return using your new name.

Now tell friends, relatives, and associates that you have changed your name and that you now want them to use only your new one. Introduce yourself to new acquaintances with your new name, too. This includes new applications for credit, insurance, and employment.

If the state in which you presently reside does not recognize the usage method, simply set up a residence in a state that has the usage provision and change your name there.

CHANGING YOUR ADDRESS

The last freedom—freedom to flee.

—Berliner Illustrirte

An essential part of escaping from the prison of your past records is the changing of your address. The address is an important part of the identification systems used by the major credit bureaus.

According to the United States Postal Service (USPS), a residence address is defined as anywhere you live, have lived, can stay the night at, and receive mail at in regard to any of the foregoing. So, if you can receive mail at and have the ability or approval to stay the night at the address you list on the credit application as your present residence address, then it is a residence address as defined by the authority on addresses in this country, the USPS.

Though a credit report may only list up to three previous addresses, the credit bureau may have up to ten previous addresses in their system. Creditors often request you to supply them with previous addresses if you have not been at your current address for at least five years. This information is used in conjunction with other identifying information when requesting a report from the credit bureaus to verify that the correct record is retrieved.

If privacy is your goal, don't provide the creditor with any information, such as a previous address. It will only link you to other identifying information from your past.

The best way to create a new residence is simply to move to another area with another zip code and a different street name. Moving to another state or country is even more preferable.

If moving is not practical, it is possible to use the address of a friend or relative to receive mail. When forwarding mail, you should have the friend or relative save the mail for you to pick up on an agreed schedule, or have them repackage your mail into a single large envelope and send it to you at a more convenient pickup location.

Do not have the friend or relative put your forwarding address on the individual pieces of mail and send it to you. This mail may inadvertently be returned to the sender, who will then have yet another address for your file. Besides, most credit cards, tax refund checks, new checkbooks, etc., will not be forwarded.

CHANGING YOUR SOCIAL SECURITY NUMBER

The Federal Trade Commission warns consumers to be on the alert for unscrupulous credit repair companies who offer to create a new credit file for individuals by instructing them to obtain an Employer Identification Number (EIN) from the IRS. An EIN is used by businesses for tax identification and resembles a Social Security number. According to the bulletin, these credit repair companies are instructing individuals with bad credit to use the EIN in place of their Social Security number along with a new address.

According to the Department of Health, Education, and Welfare's publication, *Records, Computers, and the Rights of Citizens*, the Social Security Act provides that "any employee may have his account number changed at any time by applying to the Social Security Board and showing good reason for the change. With that exception, only one account number will be assigned to an employee."

The following is an excerpt from the Social Security Administration's Social Security Number Policy and General Procedures Manual (instructions to employees of the SSA). Section 00205 reads in part:

Application Interview for Second SSNs

A. General

Since requests for second SSNs are considered original

applications, an in-person interview is mandatory when the individual is age 18 or older.

B. What to tell applicant

1. Potential problems with multiple SSNs

During the interview explain the potential problems associated with assigning a second number since many organizations, both public and private, may have records under the old number.

Examples:

- IRS
- banks
- Department of Motor Vehicles
- other federal and state agencies
- schools
- credit bureaus

2. SSNs will be cross-referenced

Also explain that the original SSN will remain assigned to the number holder (NH). The old and new numbers will be cross-referenced so that the earnings can be properly credited and misuse of the SSN can be prevented. The information on both numbers is confidential unless disclosure is required by law or allowed by the NH. Explain that we will not void, delete, or cancel the original SSN.

Section 00205.030 reads in part:

Required Documentation

A. Applicant's statement

Get the individual's signed statement (Form SSA-795) explaining the reasons for wanting a second SSN.

NOTE: If the reason is listed in RM 00205.040 A., explain that it is not a valid reason to assign a second SSN. If the individual insists on applying, see RM 00205.040 B.

B. Report of contact

Prepare a report of contact (Form SSA-5002) to document the interview. Include your observations and/or reactions to the individual's allegations.

C. Evidence of problem

1. General

Ask the applicant to submit documentary evidence showing how the SSN is disadvantaging him/her and that he/she is not at fault. This shall include third party cooperation of the problem, if possible (e.g., police report regarding misrepresentation by another individual using the NH's SSN). If there is no evidence, the applicant's statement must give the full reason for the request.

2. Applicant alleges that credit record is affected.

When the applicant alleges that someone has used his/her SSN to gain access to and/or affect his/her credit, ask the applicant for copies of the credit record, correspondence showing the applicant's attempts to correct the credit record, and other evidence supporting the allegations. A statement from the credit bureau and/or creditors should show:

— how the applicant's SSN was used,

(If the applicant already has one or more SSNs on record, advise the applicant to use the cross-referred multiple. See RM 00205.020E.)

- harassment/abuse by ex-spouse or others
- death threats or stalking
- misuse of SSN to fraudulently obtain credit, public benefits, employment, etc.

Section 00205.040 reads in part:

OF Denials of Second SSN Requests

A. When OF should deny second SSN requests

Deny the request if the individual gives one of the following reasons:

- avoidance of the law or legal responsibility
- poor credit record when the applicant is at fault (When the applicant is not at fault, see RM 00205.030.)
- bankruptcy
- lost or stolen SSN card and there is no evidence of misuse
- desire for a specific number
- use of SSN by other government agencies and/or by private companies
- fails to submit documentary evidence which should be available (RM 00205.030)

Summary of Official Requirements
for Changing SSN

1. Determine your reason for requesting a second SSN.
2. Obtain corroborating evidence to prove how the SSN is disadvantaging you at no fault of your own.
3. Complete a form SS-5 (available at all SSA offices).
4. Present all documentation to the Social Security office (preferably a supervisor).

– that the applicant was not responsible, and
– how a new SSN would prevent further unauthorized access.

NOTE: Such requests for a second SSN cannot be approved by the OF. When the required documentation has been obtained, submit it to ORSI for review with a completed SS-5, per RM 00205.045 B.

3. Earnings discrepancy or scrambled earnings problem

When a second SSN is needed to resolve an earnings discrepancy or scrambled earnings problem under the rules in RM 03870.050, document the file with evidence to justify the action.

Examples:

– earnings discrepancy file records
– IRS correspondence
– OCRO correspondence (e.g. SSA-5533-U3 requesting development)

The evidence should also clearly identify the original NH and show why a second SSN is being issued to that individual rather than to the person improperly using the SSN.

Section 00205.035 reads in part:

OF Approval of Second SSN Requests

A. When OF can approve second SSN request

Approve the request only if the reason given is one of those listed below and supporting evidence is convincing. Assign a second SSN through District Office Direct Input (DODI).

Response time for approval or denial may vary from area to area or office to office. The average time for receiving a new SSN is three to four weeks.

NOTE: Do not seek a name change and a second SSN at the same time as it may arouse suspicion on the part of the SSA. You may change your name on your Social Security card if desired with very little effort after you have received your new SSN.

SSN Cross-Referencing

A news release dated April 13, 1989, from the U.S. Department of Health and Human Services quoted Dorcas R. Hardy, Commissioner of the Social Security Administration, as saying, in part:

> Since the late 1970s SSA has been routinely performing negative Social Security number verifications. By this, the agency confirms to a requestor if a particular name and SSN do not match our records. On the other hand, the agency will not confirm if they do. No other information, including wage and benefit data, is released to an outside source without the expressed consent of the individual whose record is involved.
>
> The past practice of providing negative SSN verification was permissible under both the Privacy Act and the Freedom of Information Act. However, a recent Supreme Court decision—*Department of Justice v. Reporting Committee for Freedom of the Press* of March 22—addressed this complex issue and has significantly narrowed the circumstances under which information on individuals can be released.
>
> Last year, EXPERIAN Credit Data requested negative verifications for 140 million cases in their credit files. The EXPERIAN request was larger than, but otherwise similar to, requests that the agency has filled in the past.

SSN Is Not Required By Law

Individuals who have previously encumbered their lives with unwanted data records can now end their slavery to the system. They can escape—and close their SSN file—by making their moral objection to the system known to the Social Security Administration. The response the Social Security Administration recently gave to "religious objector" appears on the following page.

Social Security Number Fraud

SSN fraud occurs under an extremely wide variety of circumstances. Here are just a few common examples of SSN fraud:

- using multiple bogus SSNs to receive various types of benefits under fictitious identities
- using another person's name and SSN to cash U.S. government bonds illegally
- obtaining a SSN under false pretenses
- selling bogus SSN cards as part of fake identification packages, in connection with illegal immigration and other schemes
- presenting fraudulent evidence to obtain a SSN
- making, possessing, buying, or selling counterfeit SSN cards
- using another person's name and SSN to receive benefits on that person's record
- using fraudulent SSNs to set up fictitious credit histories and to apply for bank loans
- using a bogus SSN to receive medical benefits
- working under an incorrect SSN to conceal income while receiving disability insurance benefits, retirement insurance benefits, supplemental security income, or welfare payments
- using a bogus SSN to conceal receipt of Veterans Administration payments
- using bogus SSNs to file fraudulent requests for tax refunds (multiple-filer scheme)
- using bogus SSNs to obtain a "circuit-breaker" refund under

The Social Security Administration does not require that you have a Social Security number. We can issue a number to you only if you submit an application showing identifying information and if you submit evidence of age, identity and citizenship.

The Social Security number you received was assigned to you on the basis of a valid application and supporting evidence, and we cannot void the record. Even though we cannot void your record, we have destroyed the Social Security card which you returned to us, and we will not release information about your number without your consent.

Your Social Security number and record will not be used at all unless you yourself activate it for employment or other purposes.

When a person is assigned a Social Security number, the primary purpose of the number is to record that person's earnings. Once a number is assigned, the Social Security Administration has no control over who might request a person to provide their number. Neither does the Social Security Administration have the authority to require an organization to provide or deny service to anyone who refuses to disclose their number.

You should request present and future employers to enter the phrase "Religious Objector" in the space provided for a Social Security number when they report your wages and taxes.

You may show this letter to your employer(s) to show that your request is valid.

Based on regulations published by the Internal Revenue Service, Social Security numbers are required on income tax forms as the tax payer identification number. If you are required to file an income tax return, we suggest you contact the Internal Revenue Service in your area to explain your position, and they will advise you on what procedures you should use.

We are unable to return the Social Security application which you completed. However, that application form will be destroyed eventually because our procedures require that all Social Security number applications be destroyed after a period of time. As requested, we have enclosed a copy of your four-page letter for your records.

Again I want to re-emphasize that your record will not be used unless you yourself decide to activate it, and we will not release any information about your number without your consent.

Sincerely,

Social Security Administrator

Religious Objector Response Letter

a state program that helps low-income elderly and disabled retain private housing
- using bogus SSNs to illegally obtain food stamps
- using bogus SSNs and false identities to apply for unemployment compensation
- using bogus SSNs to obtain Federal Worker's Compensation payments
- using a bogus SSN to obtain a federally guaranteed student loan

How SSNs Are Fraudulently Obtained

The SSN and the SSN card are often used in criminal schemes involving fraudulent identity. Usually, the SSN card is only one part of a large packet of false identification documents used in such schemes.

Otherwise valid SSNs and SSN cards are fraudulently obtained through means which include:

- using false documents and making false statements when applying for a SSN
- buying, borrowing, or stealing another person's SSN card
- bribing a SSA employee to cause issuance of a valid SSN card, or to obtain valid SSN card stock

Counterfeit SSN cards are also used in connection with various false identity crimes. The counterfeit cards may bear real or fictitious names and SSNs.

Case Histories of SSN Fraud

In Georgia, a couple was indicted on five counts of fraudulent use of SSNs. Other charges in the 66-count indictment included mail fraud, wire fraud, credit card fraud, and drug violations. The accused allegedly used several SSNs and aliases to set up fictitious credit histories in a scheme that involved up to a million dollars in money and merchandise.

In New York, a woman pleaded guilty to having received SSI benefits under one SSN while alternately working and receiving state unemployment benefits under another SSN. She was sentenced to six months in jail and two and a half years probation and was ordered to make restitution of $19,086.

In North Carolina, a man was convicted of using his deceased brother's identity and SSN in filing a claim for Social Security benefits. The violation was discovered by the Social Security office while developing the claim. The accused was sentenced to two years probation, fined $500, and ordered to pay his court-appointed attorney fees.

A New York resident was convicted on 41 counts of criminal possession of forged instruments and one count of grand larceny. He had misrepresented himself as his father, forged his father's name to U.S. government bonds, and used his own SSN card in negotiating the bonds, which amounted to more than $43,000. He was placed on probation for five years and ordered to release the deed of his home to his father.

A New York City resident pleaded guilty to the sale of counterfeit SSN cards and Puerto Rican birth certificates. The suspect, an auxiliary police officer for the New York City Police Department, was charged after a controlled purchase was made from him. He was sentenced to 6 months (suspended) and placed on probation for 1 year.

SSA Security Measures
1. New Counterfeit-Resistant SSN Card

On October 31, 1983, the SSA began issuing new, more counterfeit-resistant SSN cards. A provision in the 1983 Social Security Amendments requires that new and replacement cards be made of bank note paper and, to the maximum extent practicable, be noncounterfeitable.

The new SSN card appears quite different from the prior card issued, although it's the same size. The front of the entire form (card and stub) has a marbleized light blue tint with the words "Social Security" in white. The entire form contains small multicolored discs. Offset and intaglio printing are used, and the card is issued on bank note paper. All of the cards are issued

the card is issued on bank note paper. All of the cards are issued from Social Security Administration headquarters in Baltimore, and the card stock is kept securely in one location.

2. Fraud Awareness

SSA has trained the Social Security field employees who take SSN applications to recognize counterfeit or altered immigration documents and other documents indicating age or citizenship. Employees are encouraged to report suspected violations to the OIG (Office of the Inspector General).

3. Electronic Process to Issue SSNs

SSA tightened controls and reviews of SSN applications through the implementation in 1982 of a new electronic process, which speeds the issuance of SSNs by transmitting the application data by wire directly from the local Social Security office to the central processing system. This new process, called District Office Direct Input, reduces the possibility of obtaining cards fraudulently by increasing the difficulty of bypassing any part of the issuance process.

4. Removal of Blank SSN Card Stock from Field Offices

The new electronic SSN issuance system (DODI) also allows the SSA to remove all blank SSN card stock from field offices where it could be lost or stolen more easily.

5. Deletion of SSN from SSN Card Stub

SSA stopped printing the SSN on the tear-off stub of SSN cards. The stubs of other individuals' SSN cards were being fraudulently used by some people to get a job or establish a false identity.

6. Specially Annotated SSN Cards

In May 1982, SSA began annotating the face of SSN cards issued to legal aliens who are not authorized to work in this country with the prominent legend "Not Valid For Employment." This is to advise employers that individuals presenting such SSN cards are not authorized to work in this country.

CHAPTER NINE

Rules of the Road

HOW TO ACHIEVE ULTIMATE PRIVACY

1. Establish an alternate identity, including new driver's license, birth certificate, Social Security card, and passport.
2. Sell services that are ordinarily not tax deductible, such as home repairs or auto repairs, and insist on payments being made in cash.
3. Don't report your income to any government agency.
4. Never open a bank account.
5. Transfer title of your house and other property to a Nevada corporation, offshore trust, or private holding company.
6. When you get phone service or other utilities in your apartment or rental house, use an alternate identity.

7. Be prepared to make large cash deposits to utility companies, since you will have no credit record. Be prepared to move without getting a refund, since they will refund your money by check.
8. Cancel all subscriptions that are in your name.
9. Leave a phony forwarding address to another country with the post office.
10. Use mail drops for your mail. You can rent several mail forwarding services in different states (or countries) and have mail sent from one to another in a random pattern. Open the accounts under different names, of course.
11. Sell your car, furniture, large appliances, and anything you can't put in storage or take with you.
12. Convert all your liquid assets to cash, slowly, then go on a Caribbean cruise.
13. Get off the boat in the Cayman Islands (or other tax haven filled with banks), take your cash in a suitcase, and open an account at a bank that has no U.S. branches.
14. Set up a foreign corporation or trust and tell your banker (face to face) to transfer your money into it. This is illegal if you don't report it to the IRS.
15. Have the trust buy property in a country that has no extradition treaty with the United States (such as Brazil).
16. Be prepared to cut off contact with your friends and relatives and live as a foreigner for the rest of your life.

LEAVING A FALSE TRAIL

Here are a number of techniques that individuals have used to disappear completely and never be found. Depending on the reasons for your "disappearance" and the urgency of your need to start over, these strategies can add several layers of additional protection to your new identity. Once again, I'd like to remind you that the author/publisher does not encourage, endorse or recommend the use of false identification for the purpose of committing fraud or evading legal obligations. The following techniques are described here for information purposes only.

- Drop dead. For a few dollars you can submit your own obituary to local newspapers. Leave copies of these notices in places where they are sure to be seen by anyone investigating your recent disappearance.
- Some people have gone so far as to file a bogus death certificate with the county recorder's office or create a fake death certificate using methods similar to the techniques used to alter or create a fake birth certificate. Blank certificates can be filled in with any information you want and then stamped and sealed with the appropriate notices. This fake death certificate can then be sent to creditors, ex-spouses, business partners, or other interested parties.
- Some people have actually started probate proceedings on themselves, using a new identity to complete the necessary paperwork. Trying to collect an insurance policy on yourself is not a good idea. Besides being blatantly illegal, you can be sure that investigators will go to great lengths to prove the claim fraudulent.
- Leave a suicide note along with some articles of clothing and identification near a large body of water with a bridge (such as the Golden Gate).
- Drop your wallet with a couple of valid credit cards in a place where it is likely to be found and used—leaving a fake trail.
- Leave a love letter behind, preferably addressed from another country.
- Purchase a one-way airline ticket to a distant country. Check in for the flight, but do not board the plane. If you have enough money, you can do this several times from different cities using different airlines and different destinations.
- Change your appearance. If you have a beard, consider a clean shaven appearance, or vice versa. If you are a bit on the heavy side and out of shape, try to lose a few pounds. You can change your body shape by working out for a few months and undergoing a strict diet. Be careful about joining health clubs, though. Don't join a club of which you were previously a member, and don't join a new club in

your old name. In fact, if you are the kind of person who frequents gyms or health clubs, you probably shouldn't work out in public at all. You might even consider putting on a few pounds to change your appearance. Hair dye, colored contact lenses, laser surgery (to eliminate tattoos, scars, or distinguishing marks), cosmetic surgery, liposuction, and other miracles of modern technology can do wonders for a quick identity change. Something as simple as a haircut or changing the way you part your hair can make you look like a different person.

- Change your style of dress. If you usually wear sweatshirts, jeans, and tennis shoes, start wearing business attire. Hats, glasses, shades, jewelry, and other accessories can turn you into a different person literally overnight. Women can change their height dramatically by changing shoes. Men can use lifts or "elevator shoes" to accomplish the same ends. In certain circles, the '60s look with bell-bottoms and platform shoes is acceptable. Your best bet, however, is to stay away from flashy or trendy outfits and try to blend in with your surroundings with clothing that does not make you stand out in a crowd. One often overlooked factor is the use of color and makeup. If blue is your favorite color and most of your wardrobe is coordinated to go with that color, consider using earth tones. Proper use of color coordination can make an amazing difference in your personal appearance.

- Drop all former contacts, including friends, relatives, business associates, church affiliations, club memberships, and magazine subscriptions. Many otherwise perfect identity changes have been thwarted due to the refusal to give up a favorite hobby or social activity. Say good-bye to your model train set, stamp collection, or bird watching society.

- Keep your mouth shut! This cannot be overemphasized. You never know who you may be talking to. Undercover agents, government informants, con artists, or even gossipy neighbors can turn one slip of the tongue into the end of your new-found freedom. Watch what you say about your past or even your future.

— On the other hand, you can deliberately leave a false trail by dropping hints about your "girlfriend" in Jamaica, your dream of going away to Zimbabwe, or your "favorite cousin's" outstanding invitation to his villa in southern France. Leave hints about a destination you never intend on travelling to.

". . . if you have been trapped by what you said, ensnared by the words of your mouth, then do this, my son, to free yourself . . ."

—Proverbs 6:2, 3

Conclusion

Once again, I'd like to advise you to use the information presented in this book with due caution. My hope is that *Super Privacy* will awaken you to a new perspective on life, offering you a variety of alternatives for financial and personal freedom.

Read this book over several times, underline important passages, and make notes in the margins. Read the books listed in the bibliography to provide you with more detailed information on specific topics. I highly recommend that you obtain a copy of the *Directory of Consumer Credit Services: The Insider's Guide to Credit Restoration, Debt Negotiation, and Financial Privacy*. The directory contains a carefully screened list of hard-to-find resources, including organizations and individuals who can help you put many of the asset protection and financial privacy strategies described in this book into action.

Feel free to write to me in care of the publisher and share your experiences, testimonials, and comments. I welcome your input regarding new strategies for financial privacy and personal freedom. Also, please let me know about new legislation, local news stories, and other information related to consumer credit, personal freedom, financial privacy, and the coming cashless society.

WARNING: The government does not want this information to be made public and could soon make this book almost impossible to distribute. Order additional copies of *Super Privacy* now for your friends and family before it's too late.

Bibliography

Allen, Gary. *None Dare Call It Conspiracy*. Concord Press, 1971.

Anonymous. *New ID in America*. Paladin Press,1983.

Asset Protection Services. Capital Asset Management, 1996.

Bamford, James. *The Puzzle Palace—Inside the National Security Agency*. Penguin Books, 1985.

———*America's Most Secret Intelligence Organization*. Penguin, 1983.

Benson, Ragnar. *Ragnar's Action Encyclopedia of Practical Knowledge and Proven Techniques*. Paladin Press, 1995.

Brette, Michael. *Offshore Services*. Capital Asset Management, 1996.

Browne, Harry. *How I Found Freedom in an Unfree World*. Avon Books, 1973.

Burkett, Larry. *The Coming Economic Earthquake*. Moody Press, 1991.

Cambist Associates, Ltd. *How to Survive and Prosper in the Next American Depression, War or Revolution*. Financial Management Associates, Inc., 1978.

Cash, Adam. *Guerrilla Capitalism: How to Practice Free Enterprise in an Unfree Economy*. Loompanics Unlimited, 1984.

Church, J.R. *Guardians of the Grail . . . and the Men Who Plan to Rule the World*. Prophecy Publications, 1989.

Cooper, William. *Behold a Pale Horse*. Light Technology Publishing, 1991.

Department of Health and Human Services, Office of Inspector General. *Social Security Number Fraud*. Eden Press.

Drake, James L. *Private Intelligence Secrets*. Alpha Publications, 1988.

Electronic Fund Transfer Systems Fraud. Paladin Press, 1989.

Hammond, Bob. *Credit Secrets: How to Erase Bad Credit*. Paladin Press, 1989.

———*Directory of Consumer Credit Services*. Capital Cities

Publishing, 1996.

———*Financial Dynamics Volume I: How to Attain Personal And Financial Privacy in the Coming Cashless Society*. Capital Cities Publishing, 1996.

———*Financial Dynamics Volume II: Advanced Strategies for Credit Restoration and Debt Crisis Intervention*. Capital Cities Publishing, 1996.

———*Financial Dynamics Volume III: How to Start and Operate Your Own Successful Consumer Advocacy Firm—From the Privacy of Your Own Home*. Capital Cities Publishing, 1996.

———*How to Beat the Credit Bureaus: The Insider's Guide to Consumer Credit*. Paladin Press, 1990.

———*Life After Debt: How to Repair Your Credit and Get out of Debt Once and For All*. Career Press, 1996.

———*Life Without Debt: Free Yourself From the Burden of Money Worries—Once and For All*. Career Press, 1995.

———*Repair Your Own Credit: Save Thousands of Dollars and Avoid the Scams*. Career Press, 1994.

Johnson, Mark T. *The Economic Guerrilla*. Paladin Press, 1987.

Johnston, Jerry. *The Last Days of Planet Earth*. Harvest House Publishers, 1991.

Jorgensen, James. *Money Shock—Ten Ways the Financial Marketplace is Transforming Our Lives*. Amacom, 1986.

Kaysing, Bill. *Privacy: How to Get It . . . How to Enjoy It*. Eden Press, 1977.

Ketcher, Michael. *The Closing Door: The End of Financial Privacy in America and How to Protect Yourself.* Institute for the Preservation of Wealth, Inc., 1992.

Kirbin, Salem. *Satan's Mark Exposed.* Salem Kirbin, Inc., 1981.

Kusserow, Richard P., Inspector General. *Birth Certificate Fraud.* Loompanics Unlimited, 1985.

Lapin, Lee. *The Outlaw Reports: Insider Secrets and Tricks of the Trade.* Paladin Press, 1993.

Lugar, Jack. *Counterfeit ID Made Easy.* Loompanics Unlimited, 1990.

Martin, James S. *Scram—Relocating Under a New Identity.* Loompanics Unlimited, 1993.

Money Laundering: The U.S. Response & Treasury's Financial Crimes Enforcement Network. FinCEN.

Nestmann, Mark. *How to Achieve Personal and Financial Privacy in a Public Age.* LPP, Ltd., 1993.

———*How to Open a Foreign Bank Account Close to Home.* Soundview Publications, 1992.

Newborn, Tony. *Secrets of International Identity Change: New ID in Canada, England, Australia, and New Zealand.* Paladin Press, 1989.

Newman, John Q. *Heavy Duty New Identity.* Loompanics Unlimited, 1991.

North, Gary. *Government by Emergency.* American Bureau of Economic Research, 1983.

Orwell, George. *1984*. Harcourt, Brace & World, Inc., 1948.

Pugsley, John A. *The Alpha Strategy*. Stratford Press, 1980.

Quigley, Carol. *Tragedy and Hope—A History of the World in Our Time*. The MacMillan Company, 1966.

Reid, Barry. *ID By Mail*. Eden Press, 1996.

Rice, Jonathan and Francis Ciabottoni. *How to Survive and Profit From the Coming Currency Recall*. Liberty Tree Press, 1986.

Richmond, Doug. *How to Disappear Completely and Never Be Found*. Loompanics Unlimited, 1986.

Rowley, Derek G. *The Nevada Corporation Handbook*. The Corporation Strategist, Inc., 1996.

Sands, Trent. *Reborn in the U.S.A.—Personal Privacy Through a New Identity*. Loompanics Unlimited, 1991.

Skousen, Mark. *Mark Skousen's Complete Guide to Financial Privacy*. Alexandria House, 1982.

Smith, Chuck. *What the World Is Coming To*. The Word for Today, 1980.

Smith, Robert Ellis. *Our Vanishing Privacy—and What You Can Do to Protect Yours*. Loompanics Unlimited, 1993.

Starchild, Adam. *Using Offshore Havens for Privacy and Profits*. Paladin Press, 1994.

The Paper Trip I & II. Eden Press, 1987.

About the Author

Bob Hammond is a nationally recognized writer, consultant, and consumer advocate. He is the author of several books on consumer credit, including *Credit Secrets, How to Beat the Credit Bureaus, Life After Debt, Repair Your Own Credit,* and *Life Without Debt.* He is the editor of the *Directory of Consumer Credit Services* and publishes *The Credit Report,* a monthly newsletter on consumer credit, financial privacy, and the coming cashless society.

A highly sought-after speaker, Hammond has been a guest on hundreds of radio and television talk shows throughout the country. In addition to conducting seminars and lectures on issues relating to consumer credit and the coming cashless society, he has provided consulting to countless individuals, civic groups, business organizations, and government agencies.

Hammond is Executive Director of Citizen's Rights Council, a nonprofit consumer education organization that provides free and low-cost information related to consumer credit and financial privacy.

He is also president of Financial Dynamics, a financial services firm providing asset protection plans, business consulting, credit restoration, debt negotiation services, and mortgage loans. His popular Financial Dynamics course has helped thousands of people get out of debt, restore their credit, and become financially independent.

Hammond received his B.A. in psychology and sociology from the University of the State of New York, Regents College, and studied screenwriting at the Hollywood Scriptwriting Institute. He is currently working on a novel, a techno-thriller about alternate identities.

Hammond is also the host of America OnLine's "Ask Dr. Privacy" on Tuesday nights at 9:00 EST. (On AOL, go to keyword: MoneyWhiz.) Also, check out his web site at http://www.drprivacy.com and Paladin Press' web site at http://www.paladin-press.com.

If you wish to contact Bob Hammond, please write to him in care of Paladin Press, P.O. Box 1307, Boulder, CO 80306, or e-mail him at Drprivacy@aol.com.